Skills in Sociology

Dan Pritchard

Causeway Press

Dedication   Moira and Jennifer

Mike Haralambos and all at Causeway, Rod White, Jeff Hale, John Belcher, Mike Walters, Coleford Library, Whitecross Resource Centre, Royal Forest of Dean College Library, Alan Jenkins, Chris Vidler, Duncan Hatcher, Chris Brain, Hayley Fisher, Sheryl Burt, Danny Myers, Trevor Davies, Mike Martin, Sally Higgins, Perry Gardener, Chris and Byron Richards, John, Viv, Michael and Mathew Edwards, Kevin Greenough, John Green, June Abram, Dave, Barbara and Mary Powell, Peter Rawes, and all my Sociology classes past, present and future.

Design and cover   Susan and Andrew Allen

Artwork   John Belcher, p.18; Sandy Britton-Finnie pp.56, 92.

Typing   Ingrid Hamer

Picture credits   Brick. p.33; Central TV. p.13 (left); Compassion in World Farming p.73; Daily Mirror pp.17 (top), 75 (right); D. C. Thompson pp.22, 31, © D.C. Thompson & Co. Ltd., 1989; Express Newspapers pp.23, 32 (bottom), 89; Greenpeace p.72; Institute of Race Relations pp.60, 61, 62 (top); Ladybird Books p.21 (top), from a former edition of *Things we do* published by Ladybird Books Ltd, Loughborough, with the permission of the publishers; Liverpool Daily Post & Echo pp.13 (right), 41 (middle), 66, 83; Mary Evans Picture Library pp.36, 51, 68, 85 (top), 94; Mike Walters p.24; Network pp.4 (Laurie Sparkham), 28, 44 (John Sturrock), 64, 72, 87 (Mike Abrahams); NSPCC p.15; Peter Rawes p.50; Popperfoto pp.8, 9, 10 11 (top), 43, 49; Punch pp.41 (top left), 76, 84, 85, reproduced by permission of Punch; Rex Features p.87 (bottom); Sally & Richard Greenhill pp.27, 63, 79, 81, 90 (top); Topham Picture Library pp.11 (bottom), 55, 90 (bottom), 93; United Media p.14; PEANUTS Characters: Charlie Brown © 1950, United Feature Syndicate, Inc., Linus © 1952, United Feature Syndicate, Inc., p. 25 PEANUT Characters: Charlie Brown © 1950, United Feature Syndicate, Inc., Lucy © 1952, United Feature Syndicate, Inc.

Text, tables, charts (sources acknowledged in text)   Compassion in World Farming p.73; Daily Mirror p.6; HMSO pp.19, 24, 44, 45, 78, 88, reproduced with the permission of the Controller of HMSO; Ladybird Books p.21, from a former edition of *Things we do* published by Ladybird Books Ltd., Loughborough, with the permission of the publishers; NSPCC p.15.

Every effort has been made to locate the copyright owners of material used in the book. Any omissions brought to our attention are regretted and will be credited in subsequent printings.

Causeway Press Ltd.
PO Box 13, Ormskirk, Lancs. L39 5HP

© Dan Pritchard 1989
1st Impression 1989

British Library Cataloguing in Publication Data
Pritchard, Dan
Skills in sociology
1. Sociology
I. Title
301
ISBN 0–946183–56–2

Typesetting by Lloyd Williams, Southport
Printed and bound by The Alden Press, Oxford.

Contents

Section 1
SOCIALISATION

1 Differences in socialisation

Introduction

The aim of this unit is to help you to understand how four boys, each born in the United Kingdom, can behave very differently.
Data 1.1 is about a 12 year old boy who grew up in Belfast. The photograph (1.2) shows the types of pictures painted in Catholic areas of Belfast by supporters of the IRA (Irish Republican Army).

Blood Brothers (1.3) is an extract from a play about twins who were separated at birth. One is raised in a poor working class family, the other in a well-off middle class family. The extract from *Tarzan of the Apes* (1.4) is from a novel about an English boy raised by chimpanzees in a tropical rain forest in Africa.

Growing up in Belfast   1.1

A 12 year old boy I visited in Belfast sat on a couch with his mother and pointed to the red crease where the British plastic bullet entered his jaw. When I asked him what he intended to do when he grew up he answered after some thought that he might wish to join the IRA.

Source: Roger Rosenblatt, *Children of War*

1.2

IRA wall painting

'Blood Brothers'   1.3

Mickey: Gis a sweet

Edward: All right (He offers a bag from his pocket).

Mickey: (trying to work out the catch, suspiciously taking one): Can I have another one. For our Sammy?

Edward: Yes, of course. Take as many as you want.

Mickey: (taking a handful): Are you soft?

Edward: I don't think so.

Mickey: Around here if y' ask for a sweet y' have to ask about 20 million times. And y' know what?

Edward: What?

Mickey: They still don't bleedin' give you one. Sometimes our Sammy does but y' have to be dead careful if our Sammy gives you a sweet.

Edward: Why?

Mickey: Cos if our Sammy gives y' a sweet he's usually weed on it first.

Edward: (exploding in giggles): Oh! – that sounds like great fun . . . Do you want to come and play?

Mickey: I might do. But I'm not playing now cos I'm pissed off.

Edward: (awed): Pissed off. You say smashing things don't you? Do you know more words like that?

Mickey: Yeh, yeh, I know loads of words like that. Y'know like the 'F' word.

Edward: (clueless): Pardon?

Mickey: The 'F' word.

(Edward is still puzzled. Mickey looks around to check that he cannot be overheard, then whispers the word to Edward. The two of them immediately wriggle and giggle with glee).

Edward: What does it mean?

Mickey: I don't know. It sounds good though doesn't it?

Edward: Fantastic. When I get home I'll look it up in the dictionary.

Mickey: In the what . . .?

Source: Willy Russell, *Blood Brothers*

Tarzan of the Apes

As Tarzan grew he made rapid strides so that by the time he was 10 years old he was an excellent climber . . .

In many ways did he differ from them (the chimpanzees) and they often marvelled at his superior running.

From early childhood he had used his hands to swing from branch to branch after the manner of his giant mother and as he grew older he spent hour upon hour daily speeding through the tree tops with his brothers and sisters . . .

He could spring 20 feet across space at the dizzy heights of the forest top.

He could drop 20 feet at a stretch from limb to limb in rapid descent to the ground.

His life among those fierce apes had been happy: for his recollection held no other life, nor did he know that there existed within the universe aught else than his little forest and the wild jungle animals with which he was familiar.

Source: Edgar Rice Burroughs, *Tarzan of the Apes*

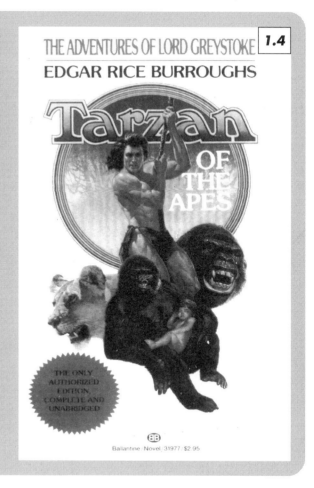

THE ADVENTURES OF LORD GREYSTOKE 1.4
EDGAR RICE BURROUGHS
Tarzan OF THE APES

THE ONLY AUTHORIZED EDITION, COMPLETE AND UNABRIDGED

Ballantine / Novel / 31977 / $2.95

Questions

1. Why do you think the Belfast boy (1.1) considered joining the IRA?

2. How might paintings, such as the one shown in data 1.2, influence the boy's attitude towards the IRA?

3. In the extract from *Blood Brothers* (1.3), which of the boys was raised in a working class family, which in a middle class family? Give reasons for your answer.

4. Why was Tarzan (1.4) an 'excellent climber'; how did he learn 'to swing from branch to branch'?

5. Human beings learn their behaviour. This process is known as socialisation. People brought up and socialised in different ways will behave differently. Using data 1.1 - 1.4, write a short essay supporting these statements.

Coursework idea

Interview somebody who has been socialised differently from yourself, eg someone of different age, class, ethnicity and/or gender. Try to discover the similarities and differences between them and yourself in terms of behaviour, attitudes and beliefs. See if you can find out how far these similarities and differences are due to the ways in which you have each been socialised.

Introduction

The aim of this unit is to show that in order to become a normal member of society, a child needs to be socialised by other human beings. There are a number of examples of children raised by animals - some true, some fictional such as Tarzan of the Apes. For instance, there are reports of children raised by wolves from as far apart as France and India. The following newspaper article deals with a young boy from West Germany and his 'mother', an alsatian. The article on the facing page looks at a girl raised in unusual circumstances - kept in seclusion by her mother who was a deaf-mute.

Horst   2.1

HE EVEN COCKED HIS LEG JUST LIKE A DOG

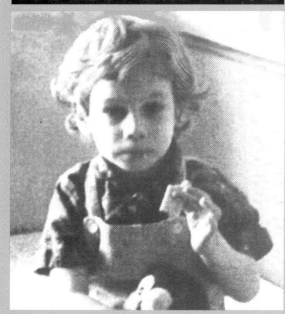

REBORN: Horst sits up, cuddling a soft toy, just like a normal child.

turned her affections to the new baby.

Asta nuzzled him, licked his hands, face and bottom clean, kept him warm in a furry blanket under her tummy.

Horst's grandmother Elisabeth said: "I saw how the dog's mothering instinct was transferred to the boy. She never left his side and growled when anyone came near."

And the caretaker at the flats in Mettmann, West Germany, said:

"They touched and stroked each other. The dog was the only one who gave him anything like love."

Meanwhile the parents left them in squalor. They gave Asta meat and water. They put bananas, milk and porridge on a table for Horst.

Then the door slammed on the two-roomed flat and they were off out to the pub or a disco.

Growled

They have said: "He had everything he needed. In fact he had more than most - he had Asta."

It seems they didn't notice that their son was growing more and more like a dog.

He whimpered and growled instead of talked. He preferred crawling to walking. He slept curled up like a puppy, his head between his "paws".

One day Horst, dressed only in pyjamas, was found tottering in the road.

Asta was nudging him with her nose to help him stand.

As a result, Horst's father took the handles off the doors to stop him escaping again.

Horst and Asta were confined to one room.

And when they were discovered there, sharing a raw chicken, Horst's extraordinary existence came to light.

The wallpaper was clawed into tatters. There was a kennel stench. Scraps of old food were scattered round.

DEVOTED: Horst's "mum", Asta

By DENNIS NEWSON and ROGER TODD

Horst's cot was unused, a film of grime over the quilt, while on the floor lay their blanket bed. There were no toys save a squeaky rubber rabbit.

Now Horst Werner Reinhard is in a clinic in Wuppertal being reborn.

He can keep down hot food - which he had never had - and he has added weight to his feeble frame, a third underweight.

The staff are talking to him, slowly teaching him to accept and enjoy cuddles, smiling at him, showing him toys and encouraging him to explore his new world.

And he's learning that humans can be loving too.

Source: *Daily Mirror,* 24.3.88

Shocking truth of the puppy boy

PUPPY boy Horst is three years and four months old - and just beginning his life as a human being.

He is the child raised by a devoted pet Alsatian called Asta while his parents went out drinking.

He became so like a dog that he didn't know how to use a toilet - and cocked his leg against a bush instead.

Now, as Horst gradually learns the behaviour of a normal little boy, the full shocking story of his lost babyhood is slowly being unravelled.

Alsatian Asta had a litter of eight puppies just before Horst was born in November 1984 and they were taken from her.

Pining for her brood, the dog

Isabelle

Isabelle was an illegitimate child and had been kept in seclusion for that reason. Her mother was a deaf-mute and it appears that she and Isabelle spent most of their time together in a dark room. As a result Isabelle had no chance to develop speech; when she communicated with her mother it was by means of gestures. At first it was even hard to tell whether or not she could hear, so unused were her senses. Many of her actions resembled those of deaf children.

The individuals in charge of her launched a systematic and skilful programme of training. The task seemed hopeless at first but gradually she began to respond. After the first few hurdles had at last been overcome, a curious thing happened. She went through the usual stages of learning characteristic of the years from one to six not only in proper succession but far more rapidly than normal. In a little over two months after her first vocalisation she was putting sentences together. Nine months after that she could identify words and sentences on the printed page, could write well, could add to ten, and could retell a story after hearing it. Seven months beyond this point she had a vocabulary of 1,500-2,000 words and was asking complicated questions. Starting from an educational level of between one and three years (depending on what aspect one considers), she had reached a normal level by the time she was eight-and-a-half years old. In short, she covered in two years the stages of learning that ordinarily require six. Or, to put it another way, her IQ trebled in a year and a half.

She eventually entered school where she participated in all school activities as normally as other children.

Source: K. Davis, *Human Society*

Questions

1. Name three items of behaviour that Horst learned from Asta.
2. Why do you think he learned to behave in these ways?
3. Why does the article state that 'Horst is . . . just beginning his life as a human being'?
4. Isabelle was a perfectly normal child raised in abnormal circumstances. Briefly outline the evidence which supports this statement.
5. Human behaviour is learned rather than inborn or genetically determined. Discuss this view with some reference to Horst and Isabelle.

Coursework idea

Find examples of children raised in unusual circumstances. Discuss what they show about how human beings learn their behaviour and what it means to be human.

3 Other cultures

Introduction

In this unit you will see how people in other parts of the world behave differently from ourselves. This is because they have been socialised into different cultures.

Veronica Doubleday (3.1 and 3.2) is a journalist who has visited Afghanistan several times. She tried to fit in with Afghan culture but found it difficult to change her behaviour.

Data 3.4 describes a custom from the New Hebrides (islands in the Pacific). Some years ago the Duke of Edinburgh watched open-mouthed as men practised the 'leap from the tower nest'.

Living in Afghanistan   3.1

The women asked me about England. How far was it? How far away was it? How could it be so far by road and so close by plane? What were our houses like? What food did we eat? How could we bear to eat potatoes every day and not rice? Was it true we believed in true love? How could a boy and a girl choose one another? Was it not better for a mother to choose a bride for her son? They were lively and curious yet narrow in their outlook. Like many Heratis they could not read and they had not attended secular (non-religious) school. They did not read books or newspapers: at that time there was no television in Afghanistan: they did not go to the cinema or theatre. Their knowledge and entertainment came from visiting and being visited by other women and from ritual gatherings, particularly weddings.

Sometimes they invited me to lunch. The men came home to eat and were always served first, sitting apart from the women and children. I would be given a separate tray of food and thoughtfully supplied with a spoon since I could not eat efficiently with my fingers.

Source: Veronica Doubleday, *Three Women of Herat*

Learning to belong   3.2

Veiled, I became like a Muslim woman and accepted lower status: I walked more slowly and gently, slipping quietly along streets and alleyways, and merging into my surroundings.

Source: Veronica Doubleday, *Three Women of Herat*

3.3

Muslim woman in Afghanistan

3.4

Risking death with every jump, the men of the New Hebrides display their courage and daring by throwing themselves from a tower secured only by a liana (a rope made from a climbing plant). The children and old men jump from a height of a few yards, the men from higher up and even from the summit. Sometimes the elasticity stretches the liana longer than was expected and the man is slammed hard against the ground. At least once a year a man must show that he is a man.

Source: Folco Quilici, *Primitive Tribes*

Questions

1. On the basis of Data 3.1 briefly state how a woman from Afghanistan would react to her first day in England. Give reasons for your answer.
2. Veronica Doubleday felt 'more at home' when she wore a veil in Afghanistan. Why do you think she felt like this?
3. If you were male and raised in the New Hebrides, you would probably jump from the 'tower nest'. Why?
4. Give an example from the West of 'proving manhood'.

Coursework idea

Study a small scale, pre-literate society (eg an Eskimo, Australian Aborigine or American Indian society). Compare this society to your own in terms of 1) how young people are socialised and 2) what young people are taught.

4 Socialisation for life and death

Introduction

People usually take the things they learn during socialisation for granted. They do not realise just how much of their lives - and, in the examples given below, their deaths - are influenced and shaped by socialisation. Data 4.1 (from a novel about India from the 1850s to the 1870s) looks at the practice of 'suttee' when a Hindu widow burned herself to death on her husband's funeral pyre.

Data 4.2 examines the code of honour of the Samurai warriors in traditional Japanese society. Data 4.3 shows how this tradition of death before dishonour continued in World War II with Japanese Kamikaze ('suicide') pilots.

Suttee

4.1

To the sound of that chanting she began to walk around the pyre circling it three times as once on her wedding day and wearing this same dress. She had circled the sacred fire, tied by her veil to the shrunken thing that now lay waiting for her on a bridal bed of cedar-logs and spices. She arranged the wide folds of her scarlet dress so as to show it to its best advantage, and then gently lifted the dead man's head onto her lap settling it with infinite care, as though he were asleep and she did not wish to wake him.

The boy's hands, guided by the Brahmin's (the priest), lowered the torch until it touched the pyre near the feet of the dead man. Bright flowers of fire sprang up from the wood and blossomed in orange and green and violet . . . the priest took the brand from him and went quickly to the other end of the pyre and touched it to the logs at the suttee's back. A brilliant tongue of flame shot

skyward and simultaneously the crowd found its voice and once again roared its homage and approval.

Source: M.M. Kaye, *The Far Pavilions*

Officially banned for over 150 years, suttee is still occasionally practised, as seen in this photograph from 1977.

The Samurai

4.2

A Samurai was expected to die for his lord if necessary and there could be no question of surrender if defeated in battle.

Rather than lose his honour the Samurai was expected to commit *suppuku* or *harikari*, the ritual sacrifice of one's life by cutting deeply into and across one's stomach, with a fellow Samurai shortening one's agony by slicing off the head with a single stroke of the sword.

Source: Richard Sims, *Modern Japan*

The first Kamikaze

October 13, 1944, aboard the US aircraft carrier *Franklin* the crew was at action stations.
A twin seater plane with the red ball of the Rising Sun (the symbol of Japan) on both sides came hurtling towards the *Franklin*. It was going to crash on the deck. And then came the impact. An enormous explosion and the plane disappeared in a cloud of smoke.
Rear Admiral Masafumi Arima had dived to his death deliberately. Arima was the first of the Kamikazes.

Source: E.P. Hoyt, *The Kamikazes*

4.3

Kamikaze attack on the USS *Hornet*

Questions

1. Why did many Hindu women in traditional Indian society accept the custom of suttee?
2. How can the Kamikaze pilots be seen as a continuation of the Samurai tradition?
3. Name an occasion when you might risk your own life. Suggest how your socialisation has influenced you to take this risk.
4. Think of an occupation in which people risk their lives. Suggest how they might have been socialised at work to accept and take this risk.

Kamikaze pilots about to set off on their mission, 1945

Coursework idea

Interview one or more people in dangerous jobs - eg a fireman, policeman, soldier, miner. Discuss how they have been socialised at work to accept and deal with danger. In particular look at the rules they must obey, how they are taught to be a member of a team and to follow orders.

Section 2
THE FAMILY

1   The family - a positive view

Introduction

For many of us the family is the most important social group to which we belong. Many sociologists take a similar view, seeing the family as the 'cornerstone' of society. These positive views of the family are seen in extracts 1.1 and 1.2. In the first, Roald Dahl (writer of children's books) describes his first night away from his family as a 10 year old boy at boarding school.

In the second extract, from John Steinbeck's novel *Pearl*, Kino, a poor fisherman, describes what his family means to him.

The British Royal Family, often pictured as a 'wonderful institution', reinforces the positive image of family life (1.3). The media tend to reflect this view of the family as a 'good thing' in 'soaps' and advertisements.

Roald Dahl   1.1

The first miserable homesick night at St. Peter's when I curled up in bed and the lights were put out, I could think of nothing but our house at home and my mother and my sisters. Where were they? I asked from which direction from where I was lying was Llandaff? I began to work it out and it wasn't difficult to do this because I had the Bristol Channel to help me. If I looked out of the dormitory window I could see the Channel itself. Therefore if I turned towards the window I would be facing home. I wriggled round in my bed and faced my home and my family.

From then on during all the time I was at St. Peter's I never went to sleep with my back to my family. Never once did I go to sleep looking away from my family. It was a great comfort to do this.

Source: Roald Dahl, *Boy*

Kino the fisherman   1.2

In Kino's head there was a song now, clear and soft, and if he had been able to speak of it, he would have called it the Song of the Family . . .

The dawn came quickly now, a wash, a glow, a lightness, and then an explosion of fire as the sun arose out of the Gulf.

Kino heard the creak of the rope when Juana his wife took Coyotito out of his hanging box and cleaned him and hammocked him in her shawl in a loop that placed him close to her breast. Kino could see these things without looking at them. Juana sang softly an ancient song that had only three notes and yet endless variety of interval. And this was part of the family song too. It was all part. Sometimes it rose to an aching chord that caught the throat, saying this is safety, this is warmth, this is the 'Whole'.

Source: John Steinbeck, *Pearl*

The Royal Family 1.3

The Royal Family provides a model of what a family should be. There are 2 parents, 4 children (a mixture of boys and girls with boys predominating), a grandmother who has grown old gracefully and is still part of the family, and a clutch of grandchildren.

Source: *New Society*

The Boswells from 'Bread' 1.4

Questions

1. From the evidence in extracts 1.1 and 1.2, suggest why the family is a powerful means for socialising children.

2. For many people, the family provides an 'anchor in life', it is a major source of emotional support. Briefly discuss this statement using evidence from extracts 1.1 and 1.2.

3. In what ways does the Royal Family provide a model for family life? Why is the image of the Royal Family usually a positive one?

4. The Boswells in 'Bread' are constantly having family rows. Despite this the family always comes first. From what you know of 'Bread' or a similar series, briefly discuss how the family is presented in a positive light.

Coursework idea

Look at the way the family is shown in advertisements on television and in newspapers and magazines. How is the family presented - in a positive or negative way, as happy or unhappy etc? Why do advertisers portray the family in a certain way?

Introduction

Sociologists have been criticised for taking a one-sided view of the family and ignoring its negative side. Conflicts within the family can affect its members for the rest of their lives. The first two extracts indicate some of the problems that can arise between parents and children. The destructive effect that poverty can have on family life is outlined in extract 2.4. The problem of child abuse (2.5) has only recently been recognised. In its first year, Childline (started in 1986) received 186,000 calls from children and dealt with 22,000 serious cases of child abuse.

Father and son   2.1

I went to the sofa and held fast to it . . . My knuckles were white with the gripping, but they did not seem like my own. The cane swished and a hot line of pain cut across my buttocks. The second would be easier I told myself. But it wasn't . . . The third set my entire being into a contortion of agony. I screamed and ran away.
'Come back.'
'No.'
'Come back.'
'Please da. Please no more please.'
He chased me around the room, grabbed me and hit out again and again . . . Then in the end the bastard tried to hug me. How dare he salve his own pathetic conscience with that act of hypocrisy . . . I was filled with disgust and hated him. The hurt, the rage, the shame and the bewilderment were too deep. From that day on, my father and I were at loggerheads. He would pay.

Source: Bob Geldof, *Is That It?*

A mother's love?   2.3

Peter a 16 year old boy was finding it increasingly difficult to leave and go to school where he was expected to do well in 'A' levels. He felt he had never been an independent person at all. His mother . . . tended to comment on everything he did, every move he made, everything he ate. She seemed to be aware of what he thought. He was aware of an anxiety that flooded over him and made it difficult for him to get up in the morning to go to school or do his homework.

Source: Lynn Segar, *What's To Be Done About The Family?*

2.2

Poverty and family life 2.4

Poor families often find themselves in a situation where one person's need for shoes can only be met at the expense of another's need for a winter coat, or a man's desire for a drink and a gamble can only be satisfied at the expense of his family's food or fuel.

There are . . . pressures towards family breakdown in modern media-dominated societies; unrealistic expectations of personal happiness. Added to these the sources of conflict in poor families are legion: disputes over spending priorities . . . unpaid bills . . . unemployment stimulates rows over responsibilities, sex roles, standards of house-keeping . . . Bad housing generates arguments over who is to blame and how it can be remedied, over space for hobbies, homework, washing, noise . . . Thus all the inequalities of society weighing down on the lower strata turn the family into a battleground . . . Thus the poor family is more likely to be divided against itself, more likely to split up, less likely to be capable of successfully socialising the family.

Source: Paul Harrison, *Inside the Inner City*

Questions

1. Why might conflict within the family be extremely serious, particularly for a child's future? Discuss with reference to data 2.1.

2. A child can be smothered by its parents' love and concern. Comment on this statement with reference to data 2.2 and 2.3.

3. In an interview in *Woman's Own* Margaret Thatcher said, 'Bringing up a family is the most important thing of all'. In view of this what should the government do about poverty? Explain your answer using information from data 2.4.

4. Why were the 'emotional scars' on Sarah and Jo so deep (2.5)?

Sarah and Jo 2.5

Sarah was 15 and her younger sister, Jo, 13 when the girls told their older brother, Michael, that their father had been sexually interfering with them. The NSPCC and the police were called in immediately and the girls were taken to a place of safety. Following legal proceedings by the NSPCC the girls were placed under an Interim Care Order and went to live with foster parents.

Our caseworker found out that the girls had been sexually abused since they were very young. Their father fondled them, used sexually explicit language and, as they got older, had full sexual intercourse with them.

Their mother knew what was going on but felt unable to help. In fact, she threatened to kill the girls if they told anyone what their father was doing. But in the end they could keep quiet no longer. They were desperate.

Eventually the girls' father admitted the sexual offences which meant his children didn't have to go through the harrowing experience of giving evidence against him in court. He was charged with incest and rape and jailed for four years.

The emotional scars on Sarah and Jo ran very deep indeed. Jo, in particular, had very little confidence and found it very hard to make friends. Our caseworker helped the girls to join a local counselling and therapy group for sexually abused girls and helped their mother to understand her responsibilities towards her children.

Progress with Sarah and Jo is slow — but they are improving. The girls are gradually overcoming the traumatic effects of their experience.

Source: NSPCC

Coursework idea

Write to organisations such as Childline for information about child abuse. Ask the following questions:

1) How much child abuse is there?
2) What causes it?
3) How does it affect children?
4) What should be done about it?

3 An equal partnership?

Introduction

In the early 1970s Willmott and Young conducted a survey of family life in London. In their book *The Symmetrical Family* they claim that husband and wife form an equal partnership in the family. This view has been strongly criticised. The following extracts examine part of this criticism.

A housewife's lament   3.1

Here lies a poor woman who was always tired,
She lived in a house where help wasn't hired:
Her last words on earth were: 'Dear Friends, I am going
To where there's no cooking, or washing, or sewing,
For everything there is exact to my wishes,
For where they don't eat there's no washing of dishes.
I'll be where loud anthems will also be ringing,
But having no voice I'll be quit of singing.
Don't mourn for me now, don't mourn for me never,
I am going to do nothing for ever and ever.'

Anonymous

His and hers   3.3

There are two marriages in every marital union, his and hers. And his is better than hers . . . It is men who thrive on marriage. Despite all the jokes about marriage in which men indulge, all the complaints they lodge against it, it is one of the greatest boons of their sex.

Source: Jessie Bernard, *The Future of the Family*

Tea and tranquillisers   3.2

Sunday 2nd: Thought I'd make like a good wife today, try the role for size, so to speak, so when the kids woke me up at 7 I got up and I didn't speak - judging it to be the safest course if ever I was to sustain the smiling madonna mask. When I emerged from the bedroom and saw that Katie had crayonned on the stair wall, thickly, and in orange, I did not immediately scream and scream. I led her by the hand to the scene of her crime and then I screamed and screamed.

Source: Diane Harpwood, *Tea and Tranquillisers - the diary of a happy housewife.*

Feeding the family   3.4

Work and family life   3.5

Men frequently see and experience marriage as something which supports them in the world of work, providing the domestic back-up which makes their working lives easier and even enhances their job prospects. They will expect the process to begin when they get married, often with wife taking over where mother left off and to go on uninterrupted . . .

By contrast when women get married they are likely to experience an immediate tension between the demands of their paid work outside and those of their unpaid labours in the home.

Source: *New Society*, March 1987

The breadwinner returns   3.7

Source: *Daily Mirror*

Questions

1. Many women complain about the pressures of housework and rearing children. Are their complaints justified? Refer to data 3.1 and 3.2 in your answer.

2. Research has shown that 'working wives' (those in paid employment) still have the main responsibility for housework and childrearing. In view of this, is marriage an equal partnership? Explain your answer.

3. Marriage for men 'is one of the greatest boons (advantages) of their sex' (3.3). Do you agree? Refer to data 3.3 - 3.7 in your answer.

Coursework idea

Interview married couples where both partners are in paid employment. Find out who does what in the home. Is there an equal partnership?

OR

Interview young people about their hopes and expectations for marriage. Do they look forward to an equal partnership?

4 Divorce

Introduction

Over the past 30 years the divorce rate in the UK (the number of divorces per thousand existing marriages) has risen over sixfold. The Divorce Reform Act, which came into force in 1971, made divorce quicker, easier and cheaper. It was followed by a large increase in divorce. The Matrimonial and Family Proceedings Act, which came into effect in October 1984, allowed couples to petition for divorce after one year of marriage. Previously they had to be married for three years. If the number of divorces continues at the same rate, over one in three marriages will end in divorce.

Unhappily ever after   4.1

The continuing surge in the number of divorces does not necessarily mean that there are more unhappy marriages now than before. Unhappy marriages do not invariably end in divorce. Also, there are no records of marriages which end informally by separation. And apart from financial considerations and changes in divorce law and procedure, couples' decisions to divorce are affected by public values. A marriage situation considered commonplace and unremarkable 50 years ago may be felt to be intolerable today.

Two changes in beliefs about marriage have been suggested to explain the current high rate of breakdown. One is that people have higher expectations of personal fulfilment from marriage and the other has to do with what has been called the 'symmetrical family', in which both partners work outside the home, sharing domestic tasks, although evidence shows that this equality exists more in theory than in practice. These egalitarian marriages can be more satisfying for both partners, but give rise to new tensions.

But in spite of the casualty rate, marriage is still a popular institution and the experience of a failed marriage does not deter people from marrying again. One in three marriages from 1979-81 was a remarriage for one of the partners. Couples are also redivorcing more than they did before. Redivorce figures run at roughly one-fifth the divorce rate and have doubled since 1961.

Source: *Guardian*, 17.6.86

POOR OLD GEORGE IS A BIT OUT OF THINGS NOWADAYS— HE'S ONLY ON HIS FIRST DIVORCE.

Divorce in the UK 4.2

Year	Number of divorces (decrees absolute)
1961	27,000
1971	80,000
1976	136,000
1981	157,000
1982	159,000
1983	162,000
1984	158,000
1985	175,000
1986	168,000
1987	165,000

Source: adapted from *Social Trends*, 1989

Who divorces? 4.3

Divorce rates are four times higher in social class 5 (unskilled manual) than among professional groups and highest of all amongst the unemployed.

In England and Wales in 1987, 73% of divorces were granted to wives, the highest proportion ever recorded. This figure has steadily risen over the past 40 years.

The older a couple were at marriage, the less likely they are to divorce. Those who marry in their teens are almost twice as likely to divorce as those who marry between the ages of 20 and 24.

Source: adapted from various issues of *Social Trends*

4.4

MARRIAGE GUIDANCE

" I think basically the trouble stems from you hating each others' guts."

Questions

1. The rise in divorce over the past 30 years does not necessarily mean that there are more unhappy marriages. Why not?

2. The rise in divorce does not necessarily mean that people are rejecting the institution of marriage. Why not?

3. 'Poor old George' (4.1) would be unlikely to appear in a cartoon drawn in the early 1960s. Why?

4. Briefly suggest reasons for the class, gender and age differences in divorce outlined in data 4.3.

5. Cartoon 4.4 oversimplifies a complex problem. Briefly comment on this statement.

Coursework idea

Interview people from different age groups about their attitudes towards divorce. Have their attitudes changed during their lifetimes? Is there any connection between changing attitudes and changes in the divorce rate?

Section 3
GENDER

1 Gender and the media

Introduction

The mass media contain images of males and females. These images help to shape our ideas about ourselves and each other. They suggest how boys and girls and men and women are supposed to look and behave. This unit looks at gender images in greeting cards, children's books, comics, novels and newspapers.

1.1

HAPPY BIRTHDAY
NOW YOU'RE 4

Hope your Birthday is fun
From the time it's begun.

1.2

Happy Birthday
Today You Are 4

Birth congratulation messages

1.3

A SON IS FUN
He'll keep you busy
With blankets and pins
And charm your hearts
With his boyish grins

What's more he'll make you
Proud and glad
Congratulations mother and dad.

Bet she's sugar and spice
And everything nice
A pink and petite little treasure
Your new little she
Who's certain to be
A wonderful bundle of pleasure.

Source: quoted in Mike O'Donnell, *A New Introduction to Sociology*

'Jane and Peter'

Jane likes to help Mummy. She wants to make cakes like Mummy.

"Let me help you, Mummy," she says. "Will you let me help, please? I can make cakes like you."

"Yes," says Mummy, "I will let you help me. You are a good girl."

"We will make some cakes for Peter and Daddy," says Jane. "They like the cakes we make."

Source: W. Murray, *Things We Do* (first published in 1964)

The children are at home. They make a shop. "I will be the man in the shop," says Peter.

"Then let me be Mummy," Jane says. "I want some things for the house," she says, "and then I want some things for tea."

1.5

Source: Helen Oxenbury, *Helping* (first published in 1982)

1.6

Source: Helen Oxenbury, *Helping* (first published in 1982)

Source: *The Beano*, 11.2.89

Mills & Boon

'He turned to face her, his piercing blue eyes absorbing every detail. A wry smile crept over his full lips, making his hard, square jawline seem a little softer. The wind ruffled his thick, dark hair. She shivered with apprehension. Why was he so dangerously handsome? The storm broke into a sudden violent downpour, soaking his clothes so they clung to his muscular frame. Grabbing her arm, he dragged her to shelter. Beneath his drenched shirt, his well-defined chest was more masculine than she had dared imagine. Pulling her to him, he pressed his warm lips against hers, kissing her possessively until she responded . . .'

I GET IT EVERY DAY!

THE STAR

PAGE 3 WATER BABES

Fins are fine for Chrissie

★ WOW what a water baby has swum onto Page Three today folks - curvy Christine Peake.

★ Our 22-year-old loves everything about the sea - especially the food. She's a dish with quite a few mussel-bound admirers herself.

★ They stop carping whenever she's around - and have a whale of a time admiring those fin-tastic looks.

Sarah's stirrup tease!

★ SEXY Sarah Hollett has just bought a horse. And when the 18-year-old from Essex is not setting our pulses galloping, she trots down to his stable - lucky creature!

★ Sarah is always a mane attraction when she stirrups for action on Page Three. Bet she looks just as cute in pony tails.

Things look mice for gorgeous Gail

★ EAR, folks! Cartoon-loving Gail McKenna has fallen head-over-heels in love - with Mickey Mouse.

★ The 19-year-old has a Mickey Mouse phone, a Mickey Mouse clock, and wants a Mickey Mouse picture painted on her bedroom wall.

★ She's also planning to visit Mickey in Disneyland. Just say cheese and let him snap you like this, Gail, and you'll give him a real mice time too.

The loveliest girls are always in your No 1 Sun

Questions

1. What do the greetings cards (1.1 - 1.3) 'say' about boys and girls?

2. Compare the images of gender shown in data 1.4 with those in 1.5 and 1.6. What effect might these images have on children in later life?

3. According to Minnie's mother (1.7), how should girls behave?

4. According to the Mills & Boon romance (1.8), what are men and women like?

5. You are from another society and you have come to this country to study gender roles. How would you describe the role of women on the basis of data 1.9 - 1.10?

Coursework idea

Collect material on gender from magazines, comics, newspapers, mail order catalogues and novels. Note how gender roles are presented in publications aimed at different audiences eg publications for young people, adults, males, females etc.

2 Gender and education

Introduction

Girls' education is one of the success stories of the past twenty years. At age 16, girls have done considerably better than boys in examinations. Although they do less well at 'A' level and fewer go on to higher education, female students after the age of 16 are steadily closing the gap. However, there are still important gender differences in education which place girls at a disadvantage. The material which follows looks at some of these differences.

School leavers with 'O' level passes 2.1

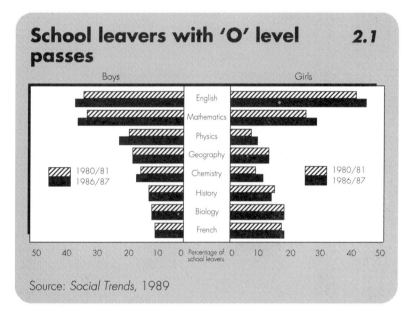

Boys   Girls

English
Mathematics
Physics
Geography
Chemistry
History
Biology
French

1980/81
1986/87

1980/81
1986/87

50 40 30 20 10 0   Percentage of school leavers   0 10 20 30 40 50

Source: *Social Trends*, 1989

Education for girls 2.3

They (my parents) obviously could not see any great advantage in my staying at school, and they were having a struggle keeping my brother at the University.
Had I been a boy any thought of my leaving school would have been discouraged immediately.
I would have been told I must make a career for myself.
I must get better qualifications.
And I would have been easily persuaded . . .
This sort of thing is continually happening to girls.
During their whole school career their parents and friends expect less of them.
They do not expect them to plan for a great career.
Education is something to make them a more socially acceptable person, and a career or job is something they pursue between leaving school and getting married.
. . . girls are encouraged to do 'suitable' subjects at school, socially acceptable subjects.
. . . girls are encouraged to do the lady-like, suitable subjects like English, history and languages, but not the sciences or mathematics which are considered more difficult and more manly subjects.

Source: Joyce Nicholson, *What Society Does To Girls*

2.2

24

Boys' own paper 2.4

The authors of texts are almost exclusively male

In the AEB's Alternative English papers, out of 16 authors, mostly of the 19th and 20th centuries, only three were women.

In the past, the excuse for choosing male authors has been that there have been so few good women writers. But now Dale Spender and Pandora Press have come to the rescue of the examiners. At the end of May, they published *Mothers of the Novel - 100 good women writers before Jane Austen.* This reveals a wealth of talent that has been ignored and hidden from women for centuries.

Questions about subjects of interest to only one sex

In the O & C English Language papers, four of the five sections are about boys' subjects. Ships, masters in a boys' school, the ritual slaughter of a shoal of porpoises, and a 'murderous patriarch' of a pike catching a chub. Of the 10 essay subjects, those likely to interest boys are: blood-thirsty nature, a man, computers, harbours, and a quotation about being a cog in a machine. Unlikely to interest either: early retirement, hurry. Might possibly be intended for girls: an inexplicable action, a female gazing at her grandmother and a story about the picture of a pig. That means three-tenths of one-fifth of the exam might have been intended for girls.

Source: Elizabeth Hendry

2.5

Questions

1. Briefly describe the trends shown in chart 2.1.

2. Look at the photographs (2.2). Are they typical of your school? Suggest why boys tend to take certain subjects and girls others.

3. Why do fewer girls than boys continue their education to age 18 and beyond? Refer to data 2.3 in your answer.

4. How are examinations biased against girls (2.4)?

5. The comic strip (2.5) makes a serious point. What is it?

Coursework idea

Count the numbers of boys and girls in your school who are taking particular subjects at examination level. Interview a sample to discover why they chose these subjects.

OR

Ask your teacher for past examination papers in English. Examine the papers for evidence of gender bias.

Introduction

Women are concentrated in certain kinds of jobs which are seen as female occupations. These jobs are usually low pay, low skill, low status occupations. Despite the Equal Pay Act (1970) and the Sex Discrimination Act (1975), women's wages have consistently remained well below the average for male workers. Despite all the talk about equal rights, many employers (and employees) are still prejudiced against women workers.

3.1

"You've been a wife and mother for twenty years — what makes you think you could handle difficult people and awkward situations?"

3.2

'I'm Gonna Be An Engineer'

3.3

You got one fault! You're a woman
You're not worth the equal pay
A bitch or a tart
You're nothing but heart
Shallow and vain
You got no brain
Go down the drain like a lady today.

Source: song by Pete Seeger

Jobs for the boys 3.4

At school I (Sally Higgins) did woodwork and motor mechanics; the teachers thought I was a 'bit daft' and that I wouldn't be able to pursue a career.

When I left school I joined the RAF and became MT (Mechanical Transport) mechanic. There are only about 45 MTs who are girls in the whole of the RAF and, in my section, there were 40 blokes and 2 girls.

A senior ranking male mechanic gave both girls in the section a rough time, telling us:-

'You are useless. I don't think females should be mechanics.'

In spite of the fact that I was rated by others as a good mechanic, eventually I retrained as a tele-communications officer.

Source: Sally Higgins (interviewed by author)

"OH! THAT EXPLAINS THE DIFFERENCE IN OUR PAY"

Building site, China

Coursework idea

Make a list of 5 typical male jobs, 5 typical female jobs, and 5 jobs which are not associated with either males or females. Ask a sample of students to choose one as their future occupation. Has their choice been influenced by gender? Interview a smaller sample in order to discover the reasons for their choice.

Questions

1. Data 3.1 - 3.3 illustrate a number of prejudices against women.
   a) What are these prejudices?
   b) How might they prevent women from having equal opportunities in employment?
2. Sally Higgins (3.4) should have received every encouragement both at school and in the RAF. Why? She has now left the RAF. Why do you think she did?
3. Pictures like data 3.6 show that many of our ideas about women and work are simply prejudices. Briefly explain why.
4. When you get down to it, data 3.5 sums up the basic reasons for gender differences in pay. Comment on this statement.

4 Gender - fighting back

Introduction

Women have been fighting for equal rights for many years - the Suffragettes in the early part of this century, the Women's Liberation Movement in the 1960s and the Feminist Movement today. They have found allies in the male half of the population but arguably the progress they have made has been largely due to their own efforts.

This unit looks at some of the ways in which women (and some men) have fought for equal rights.

Equal pay   4.1

Equal pay strike, Lyons Tea factory, Bletchley 1975

Cartoonist Posy Simmonds   4.2

28

The baby bonder   4.3

One man and his breasts: the cloth 'Baby Bonder' sells for $19.95 in the US. Its inventor, Dr. Alfred Goldson, wanted to 'improve the process of infant-bonding' and was commended in Congress for his efforts.

Source: *Male and Female*

William's doll   4.4

. . . little William wants a doll; other boys call him 'sissy', and his father brings him a basketball and an electric train. William enjoyed them but he still wants a doll. Finally his grandmother buys him a doll. 'He needs it,' she says to William's father, 'to hug and to cradle and to take to the park so that when he's a father like you he'll know how to take care of his baby.'

Source: Charlotte Zolotow, *William's Doll*

Lucky charm   4.5

A JUDGE aged 70 tells a shapely blonde teacher she should have "switched on the charm" for a policeman to avoid being booked for speeding.
Predictably, a wave of feminist fury erupts - led by Labour MP and arch kill-joy Clare Short (remember her, Page Three fans?)
We applaud the judge's comment and envy a 70-year-old who still has an eye for a pretty woman.
As for Miss Short, perhaps she should beware trying to switch on the charm if she is ever caught speeding. She'd probably end up with life!

Source: *The Sun*, Dec. 1986

Questions

1. Do you think the type of campaign shown in 4.1 is an effective way of gaining equal rights for women? Give reasons for your answer.
2. What is the point of the Posy Simmonds cartoons (4.2)?
3. Do you think the inventor of the 'baby bonder' (4.3) deserved his commendation from Congress? Give reasons.
4. Women and men need more babies like little William (4.4). Briefly discuss this statement.
5. Which view do you agree with - that of Clare Short or *The Sun* editorial (4.5)? Explain your answer.

Coursework idea

Show the Posy Simmonds cartoons (4.2) to a sample of boys and girls in your school. Ask them to interpret the message of the cartoons and whether it makes them see the roles of men and women in a different light. Compare the responses of males and females in your sample. Judge the effectiveness of the cartoons for changing attitudes about gender roles.

1 Education as social control

Introduction

One of the functions of education is to prepare young people for their role in society. This involves passing on basic values and attitudes that go beyond what is taught in lessons like English and French. Social control in schools is achieved through 'formal' methods like school rules and punishment and through 'informal' methods like teacher encouragement and school activities.

This unit looks at how some of the methods of social control in schools work. Methods used in the nineteenth century are compared with those used today and reasons for the changes are considered.

1.1

A typical lesson? 1.4

Tucker hated English. Not that that was too surprising, Tucker hated most subjects. In fact he hated almost everything to do with school. Well, not quite everything. He liked the practical subjects, and Art. He enjoyed making things. But reading old books? He could never see the point. 'I hate this rubbish,' he whispered to Tommy who was busy reading Penthouse under the desk.
Doyle was scratching his initials into the desk lid again. Benny was gazing out of the window probably dreaming about playing for England again. Cathy Hargreaves was filing her nails while Trisha Yates had her eyes closed and seemed to be asleep again.
All in all a fairly normal lesson.

Source: Phil Redmond, *Tucker and Co.*

Nineteenth century discipline 1.2

I was then sent to a boys' school to learn to 'write and cypher', thought at that time to be all the education required for poor people. The first master was a severe one, and the second was somewhat worse. On one occasion I saw him hang up a boy by this thumbs for playing truant.

Source: *The Life and Struggles of William Lovett*

Twentieth century discipline 1.3

Serious violence at Hackney Downs against teachers or other pupils is rare but only because the school has radically changed its approach to discipline. John Kemp explains: 'our kids tend to be more brusque, more suspicious of authority, more precociously self-reliant than kids from suburban areas. In the early 1970s, shortly after we went comprehensive, we tried to clamp down on disorder but the result was a number of very dramatic confrontations. You can't screw these kids down.'

Source: Paul Harrison, *Inside the Inner City*

Conforming 1.5

Friday June 5th
Miss Sproxton spotted my red socks in assembly! The old bag reported me to popeyed Scruton. He had me in his office and gave me a lecture on the dangers of being a non-conformist. Then he sent me home to change into regulation black socks.

Source: Sue Townsend, *Diary of Adrian Mole*

Source: *The Beano*

A teacher's experience *1.7*

. . . As the others finished reading the chatter started slowly building up again. After a few minutes the noise was deafening.
'Quiet,' I shouted.
No response.
'Quiet.'
'What did you say, miss?'
'The next person to speak after I count five will go straight to Mr. Lewis. One, two -.'
' - three, four -.' They all chimed in.
' - five!'
There was silence of a sort. Mouths buttoned suppressing giggles.
'Right. Now close your books.' I took up my own copy. Unfortunately I had lost the page. While I fumbled for it, a quiet voice started, ' - six, seven, eight - .' Baxter, what is the subject of the passage? Which anthropological group?'
'The staff, miss.'
'Leave the room, Baxter.'
'Yes, miss.'

Source: Ursula Bentley: *The Natural Order*

Questions

1. What is happening in 1.1? What can you work out about the attitudes of those involved from looking at their expressions?

2. How would you expect the press to react to William Lovett's account of punishment (1.2) if it were to happen today? This type of punishment was quite common in the nineteenth century. Why do you think it was possible for teachers to 'get away' with such punishments?

3. Compare the impression given of discipline in schools today by Phil Redmond (1.4) with that given for the nineteenth century (1.1, 1.2). What are the differences?

4. What reason does the writer of 1.3 give to suggest that nineteenth century methods of enforcing discipline would not work today? Why do you think this is the case?

5. What alternative methods of enforcing discipline might you expect to be used at Hackney Downs school (1.3)?

6. What does Adrian Mole (1.5) mean when he talks about a 'non-conformist'? Why is conformity seen as being so important by teachers?

7. 1.6 and 1.7 give us an impression of what may happen if rules are not applied and enforced. Using this data, construct an argument for the use of rules in school.

Coursework idea

Study and analyse the methods of social control, both formal and informal, that operate in your school/college. In each case, examine how they work and the reasons for their use. For example, work out the reasons for each of the rules and then look at how each is applied and enforced. Consider whether the rules are necessary and whether the rewards and punishments attached to the rules are effective.

Introduction

Social class is often given as the main reason for differences in educational attainment. Statistics such as those in data 2.1 are used to support this view.

However, there are other factors affecting educational performance, some of which are connected to social class, others of which are not. This unit looks at some of these factors and examines the ways in which they influence educational attainment.

2.1

Students attending university or college: by socio-economic group of father, 1984

Great Britain

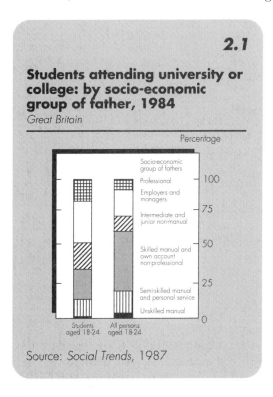

Source: *Social Trends*, 1987

Case study of a comprehensive   2.2

2TA English
Teacher: 'All right let's have some quiet.' This is shouted over the noise of the class. 'Peter I've told you once, what did I just say?'
Peter: 'If it happens next week'
Teacher: 'Right now stop talking to Sammy . . .'
Two of the girls at the back are talking and writing on a small book.
Teacher: 'Dorothy bring your books and sit here . . .'
Dorothy: 'Ugh, I'm not sitting next to him.'
She gestures at Wally.
Teachers find it almost impossible to organise discussions in 2TA's lesson and even question and answer sessions tended to deteriorate into noisy shouted responses.

2CU Chemistry
The form is silent and attentive throughout the whole of this time . . . the form is gathered round the bench at the front but are orderly without pushing one another or talking.

Distribution of social classes, forms 2TA and 2CU

	I	II	IIIN	Total non-manual	IIIM	IV	V	Total manual
2CU	5	10	5	20	12	—	—	12
2TA	2	3	2	7	15	8	3	26

Source: S.J. Ball, *Beachside Comprehensive*

Parental influence   2.3

The middle class parents take more interest in their children's progress at school than the manual working class parents do, and they become relatively more interested as their children grow older . . . the most striking difference is that many middle class fathers visit the schools to discuss their children's progress whereas working class fathers seldom do.

Source: J.W.B. Douglas, *The Home and the School*

2.4

"Morning, Froid — we hear you're the only boy who did his homework instead of watching football last night"

Language makes a difference   2.5

Responses to the teacher's question; 'Now then - have you done your homework?' 'Excuse me sir - I'm unable to hand the homework in that you gave us - I've left my books at home. I'm sorry. I'll bring it tomorrow.' (Middle class child). 'This homework thou set I've dunnin but me dad's car codn't start an I've left me book at wum.' (Rural pupil in the Forest of Dean, West Gloucestershire). 'Eh sir - that homework was dead ard like - yous ave gorra give us more time.' (Inner city pupil in Liverpool).

Source: Author

Schools matter   2.7

A study conducted by Peter Mortimore challenges the belief that a difficult social life prevents academic success.

Mortimore's researchers followed the careers of 2000 London children in 50 junior schools and took 7 years to complete.

'We found that in terms of reading progress the quality of school attended was 4 times as important as the child's age, sex or background. In maths the school was 10 times more important.'

Source: *The Guardian*

Questions

1. In what ways does 2.1 suggest that social background has an effect upon educational achievement?

2. What are the differences between the behaviour of the English and Chemistry classes in the case study in 2.2? Does this indicate that educational attainment is affected by social class? Explain your answer.

3. How do the points made in 2.3 and 2.4 help us explain the performance of pupils in school? In each case do they strengthen or weaken the argument that social class is *the* explanation for educational performance?

4. Which of the three pupils in 2.5 would you expect to be most likely to get away with not doing his/her homework? Why? How can the use of language help to explain why some pupils do better at school than others?

5. What point do you think the cartoonist in 2.6 is trying to make?

6. Does Peter Mortimore's research (2.7) reject the argument that there is a link between social background and educational success? Explain your answer fully.

Coursework idea

Look at factors other than social class which may affect educational achievement in your school/college.

You may want to consider organisation (banding, streaming etc.), discipline, peer group influences and so on.

3 Educational change

Introduction

Change in education has been a feature of the twentieth century.

During the 1960s and 1970s comprehensive schools were set up with the aim of ensuring that everyone had an equal opportunity in the education system. In the 1980s, government once again began reforming education in the hope that their reforms would meet the changing needs of economy and society. This unit looks at some of the reasons why people think that there should be educational change in the 1980s. It also looks at the problems raised by reform.

The comprehensive ideal -responses of teachers 3.1

Comprehensive education is:-
'an education which provides good opportunities for all'
'an attempt to produce a fair system'
'the breakdown of socio-economic groups to rid us of distinctions'

Source: S.J. Ball, *Beachside Comprehensive*

Schools criticised 3.3

Schools in affluent Surrey have been criticised for providing 'dull and unimaginative' education. A report by HM Inspectorate comments on 'limited expectations', preoccupation with exams and over-reliance on textbooks at secondary level. It notes narrow teaching styles, and lack of continuity between different phases of education.

Source: *Times Educational Supplement* 31.3.89

New teaching methods? 3.4

'It's very different today . . . the pupils are involved in choosing and producing their own topic of their own choice . . . No longer am I using the didactic approach (instructing the whole class) with every pupil doing the same thing at the same time.'

Source: An Airedale teacher

Science and gender 3.2

In 1987 over twice as many boys than girls passed 'O' level Physics and one third more boys than girls passed 'O' level Chemistry. More girls than boys gave up Physics and Chemistry as soon as they could. From 1989 the National Curriculum required all students to take Science in primary and secondary schools.

An effective school? 3.5

The recipe for an effective school Mortimore believes (and these findings are consistent with research in America and Australia) is as follows:
- structured sessions with a clear framework
- work-centred environment/classrooms with a business environment
- intellectually challenging teaching which includes teaching the class as a whole in an old-fashioned way.

Source: *The Guardian*, May 1988

An American comparison 3.7

It is hardly surprising that Kenneth Baker, the Education Secretary, was impressed by the schools he visited in the United States last week. Most were selective, 'magnet schools'. The Bronx High School of Science in New York, for example, is very selective indeed and gets 99% of its pupils into some form of higher education.

Source: *The Guardian*, May 1988

Kenneth Baker, Education Secretary 3.6

Are <u>you</u> going to allow him to bring back a two-tier system of schooling: one for the rich and one for the poor?

Questions

1. According to data 3.1, what are the strengths of the comprehensive system? Do you agree with these views?

2. In view of the gender differences in Science (3.2), do you agree with the changes introduced by the National Curriculum? Give reasons for your answer.

3. What criticisms are the inspectors making of schools in Surrey (3.3)? Would you expect them to approve of the methods used by the Airedale teacher (3.4)? Explain your answer.

4. Compare 3.5 with 3.4. What are the differences between these two views of good teaching? Which would you expect to be the most effective way of raising standards in education? Say why.

5. What would you say are the strengths of the American system as shown by data 3.7? How useful do you think comparisons like this are in assessing the British education system?

6. The American schools which impressed Kenneth Baker are selective - they take only the brighter pupils. What is the poster (3.6) saying? Should we bring back a 'two-tier system'? Give reasons for your answer.

Coursework idea

Collect information from the press, radio, television etc. on recent changes in education. Analyse the reasons for each change and find out what the effects have been on your school/college. Does change in education always achieve what was intended?

Section 5
Social Stratification

1 Slavery

Introduction

Slavery is one of the most rigid forms of social stratification. Slavery means the ownership of one human being by another.

Many societies have been based on slave labour - Ancient Greece and Rome, the civilisations of Central America and the Southern States of the USA.

In societies based on slavery, there are two main strata - the upper level made up of free citizens and the lower level of unfree slaves.

Ancient Rome   1.1

By about AD 300 most middle class Roman households had several slaves. The famous writer Pliny the Younger had 500 slaves, and the Emperor may have had 20,000 or more.

People could become slaves in many different ways: by being in debt, as punishment for certain crimes, or by being captured in wars. Some poor parents even sold their children as slaves, although this was against the law. Slaves' children became the slaves of their parents' owners. The gladiators were slaves. The crowds at the fights loved the combination of spectacle, bloodshed and skill. Gladiator fights were common for more than five hundred years in Rome, from about 260 BC onwards. Sometimes huge numbers died. For the one-thousandth anniversary of the founding of Rome, 2,000 gladiators were billed to die in fights between men on horseback, or in armour, or with tridents and nets, or with swords and shields.

Source: Shuter and Child, *Skills in History 1*

Roman gladiators

36

Slave auction, USA 1.2

Whipping with a paddle 1.3

Common mode of whipping with a paddle

Epitaph of a slave trader 1.4

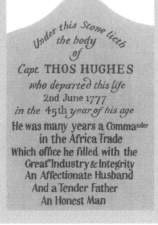

Under this Stone lieth
the body
of
Capt. THOS HUGHES
who departed this life
2nd June 1777
in the 45th year of his age
He was many years a Commander
in the Africa Trade
Which office he filled with the
Great Industry & Integrity
An Affectionate Husband
And a Tender Father
An Honest Man

4. Slaves were often treated like children. Explain this statement using data 1.3 as part of your answer.
5. Judging from data 1.4, how did many people regard the slave trade in the late eighteenth century?

Questions

1. Slaves in Rome were allowed to buy their freedom. Many who had enough money chose not to. Suggest reasons why they did not.
2. Slaves were expendable. Explain this statement using data 1.1.
3. Slaves were basically a commodity. Explain this statement using information from data 1.1 and 1.2.

Coursework idea

Study the abolition of the slave trade in Britain and/or slavery in the USA. Examine the reasons given by those who wished to keep the system and those who wanted it abolished. This will give you a valuable insight into the ideas and beliefs which maintained slavery and which led to its abolition.

Introduction

In many societies people are classified in terms of 'race'. Systems of social stratification are sometimes based on these so-called 'racial groups'. The apartheid system in South Africa is a well known example.

Apartheid means aparthood or separateness. In South Africa 'racial groups' are forced to live in separate areas. The white minority monopolises political power and owns the lion's share of the country's wealth. This unit looks at some of the inequalities of apartheid.

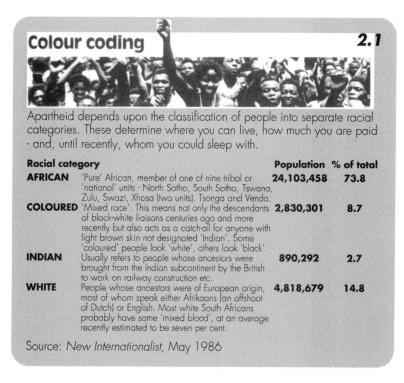

Colour coding   2.1

Apartheid depends upon the classification of people into separate racial categories. These determine where you can live, how much you are paid - and, until recently, whom you could sleep with.

Racial category		Population	% of total
AFRICAN	'Pure' African, member of one of nine tribal or 'national' units - North Sotho, South Sotho, Tswana, Zulu, Swazi, Xhosa (two units), Tsonga and Venda.	24,103,458	73.8
COLOURED	'Mixed race'. This means not only the descendants of black-white liaisons centuries ago and more recently but also acts as a catch-all for anyone with light brown skin not designated 'Indian'. Some 'coloured' people look 'white', others look 'black'.	2,830,301	8.7
INDIAN	Usually refers to people whose ancestors were brought from the Indian subcontinent by the British to work on railway construction etc.	890,292	2.7
WHITE	People whose ancestors were of European origin, most of whom speak either Afrikaans (an offshoot of Dutch) or English. Most white South Africans probably have some 'mixed blood', at an average recently estimated to be seven per cent.	4,818,679	14.8

Source: *New Internationalist*, May 1986

Inequality: from 2.2
cradle to grave

The difference between the quality of life of white people and black is enormous, and can be measured in every field from child health to average earnings.

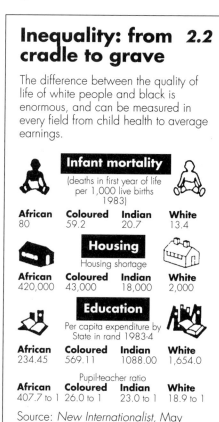

Infant mortality

(deaths in first year of life per 1,000 live births 1983)

African	Coloured	Indian	White
80	59.2	20.7	13.4

Housing

Housing shortage

African	Coloured	Indian	White
420,000	43,000	18,000	2,000

Education

Per capita expenditure by State in rand 1983-4

African	Coloured	Indian	White
234.45	569.11	1088.00	1,654.0

Pupil-teacher ratio

African	Coloured	Indian	White
407.7 to 1	26.0 to 1	23.0 to 1	18.9 to 1

Source: *New Internationalist*, May 1986

2.3

TELL HIM IT'S GETTING BETTER! HE DOESN'T BELIEVE ME !!!

Source: *Guardian*, 25.4.86

Whites only   2.4

CITY OF CAPE TOWN	STAD KAAPSTAD
NOTICE	**KENNISGEWING**
THIS BEACH IS RESERVED FOR THE WHITE GROUP ONLY.	HIERDIE STRAND IS VIR DIE BLANKE GROEP GERESERVEER.
JAN LUYT. TOWN CLERK	JAN LUYT. TOWN CLERK

Source: *New Internationalist*, May 1986

'The white man's burden?' 2.6

The whites have to justify the rape of our land, and so they claim that we are inferior. We are not worthy of God's gifts. It says so in the Bible. They lay claim to our land and our lives and then, to add insult to injury, they patronise us. They say we are ignorant children. Our salvation and welfare are - alas! - 'the white man's burden'.

And, after a while a terrible thing happens. For many of my people, the message begins to sink in. Day after day we are treated like dirt and told we are inferior. It is drummed into our heads. First, your self-respect disappears. You begin to hate everything that is black. The white culture is full of references to things that are black and evil. We are told not to let a black cat cross our path. With the war, there has come a thing called the black market, where money is traded illegally. But what black person ever heard of money before the white man came?

Source: Miriam Makeba, *Makeba, My Story*

The white world 2.7

Now that I am going out into the white world, I must be careful how I act. I do not know any white people, but I have learned how to speak to them. If a man or woman addresses me, I must answer. 'Ja, baas', which is Afrikaans for 'Yes, boss'. Always to a policeman I must say, 'Ja, baas,' or else I may end up somewhere! If a white child addresses me, I must say, 'Ja, klein baas', which is 'Yes, little boss'. I must be very careful if I want to survive.

Source: Miriam Makeba, *Makeba, My Story*

4. Apartheid is sometimes defended with the idea of separate and equal. In view of what you have read in the unit, do you think this applies to beaches (2.4), parks and other public places? Give reasons for your answer.
5. Explain the point of the cartoon strip (2.5).
6. Why are whites able to convince many blacks that blackness is inferior?
7. Blacks in South Africa are socialised to 'know their place'. Briefly explain this statement using data 2.7.

Questions

1. Only whites are permitted to vote for candidates to the South African parliament. Is South Africa a democratic society? Refer to data 2.1 in your answer.
2. Stratification systems benefit those at the top. Support this statement using information from data 2.2.
3. Data 2.3 shows South African President P.W. Botha. Briefly explain the point of the cartoon.

Coursework idea

Look at the position of ethnic minorities in the British stratification system. Analyse the similarities and differences between ethnic stratification in Britain and apartheid in South Africa.

3 Social class - a humorous view

Introduction

Social class has long been a rich source for humour - from Andy Capp, the working class hero in *The Daily Mirror,* to Margot Leadbetter, the middle class snob in *The Good Life,* to Lord Snooty in *The Beano.* These and similar portrayals of class are caricatures and stereotypes. However, they do say something about how people see class, how they feel about themselves and others in social class terms. This unit looks at humorous portrayals of class and the light they throw on the more serious side of class stratification.

3.1

"Lor, Bill, we've got into a fust-clawss carriage."
"Yer don't say so! And me wiv odd socks on!"   (1909)

3.2

Lady: "I do hope you'll get the bath done soon. It's really most inconvenient."
Plumber: "We'll do our best, lady. When's yer bath-night?"   (1932)

3.3

. . . to ensure that social status is recognised on arrival. (1947)

3.4

Pity the poor rich - crippled by taxation (1947)

"I know what they're thinking. They're thinking what a shabby old saucepan to let a boy get his head stuck into." (1951)

'Fawlty Towers'

Basil   Would you put both your names, please? . . . *(to phone)*
         Well, will you give me a date?
Melbury Er . . . I only use one.
Basil   *(with a withering look)* You don't have a first name?
Melbury No, I am Lord Melbury, so I simply sign myself 'Melbury'.
         There is a long, long pause.
Basil   *(to phone)* Go away. *(puts phone down)* . . . I'm so sorry to have kept you waiting, your lordship . . . I do apologize, please forgive me. Now, was there something, is there something, anything, I can do for you? Anything at all?
Melbury Well, I have filled this in . . .
Basil   Oh, please don't bother with that *(he takes the form and throws it away)* Now, a special room? . . . a single? A double? A suite? . . . Well, we don't have any suites, but we do have some beautiful doubles with a view . . .
Melbury No, no, just a single.
Basil   Just a single! Absolutely! How very wise if I may say so, your honour.
Melbury With a bath.
Basil   Naturally, naturally! *Naturellement!* *(he roars with laughter)*
Melbury I shall be staying for one or two nights . . .
Basil   Oh please! Please! . . . Manuel!! *(he bangs the bell)*

The cast of 'Fawlty Towers'

Questions

1. What view of the working class is given in cartoons 3.1 and 3.2?

2. The cartoon in data 3.3 is not as silly as it looks. How can social class be recognised in a graveyard?

3. Explain the irony in cartoon 3.4.

4. Cartoon 3.5 illustrates middle class snobbery. Why are the middle class in particular sometimes seen as snobbish?

5. Explain the point made in cartoon 3.6. Do you think accents matter? Briefly explain your answer.

6. Basil Fawlty's behaviour (from the TV comedy Fawlty Towers) is 'over the top'. However, it does reflect the way some people behave. Briefly describe and explain such behaviour.

Coursework idea

Collect examples of social class humour from TV, cartoons, jokes etc. Analyse your material and explain what it shows about images of social class.

4 The inequalities of class

Introduction

The material in this unit is drawn from the 1840s to the 1950s. Compared with today, social class during those years (particularly in Victorian times) was more clearly defined. The previous unit looked at the humorous side of social class. This unit takes a more serious look. It shows that class can make life more or less comfortable (4.1), it can bring happiness and distress (4.3), and even make the difference between life and death (4.2).

Class on the railways

First class

Second class

Most lines had three classes of railway carriage, though not all lines provided third class accommodation before 1844. First class carriages usually had roofs, windows and seats, but they were small and cramped. One of the main complaints about second class carriages seems to have been that they were draughty. The worst carriages, naturally, were the third class. For about 1p per kilometre, the public was allowed to travel in open trucks, the only protection from the weather being sides of about one metre in height. There were no seats, and carriage buffers were made of solid wood. Not surprisingly, people were increasingly critical of third class travel.

Eventually, Parliament intervened. In 1844, the Railways Act was passed. Amongst other things, it said that Railway Companies had to improve third class facilities.

Third class

The three classes of travel on the Liverpool-Manchester line

Source: Schools Council History 13-16 Project, *Britain 1815-51*

The sinking of the *Titanic* (1912)

Actually, there were boats for 1178 - the White Star Line complained that nobody appreciated their thoughtfulness. Even so, this took care of only 52 per cent of the 2207 people on board, and only 30 per cent of her total capacity. From now on the rules and formulas were simple indeed - lifeboats for everybody. And it was the end of class distinction in filling the boats. The White Star Line always denied class distinction - and the investigators backed them up - yet there's overwhelming evidence that the steerage (Third Class) took a beating - the *Titanic's* casualty list included four of 143 First Class women . . . 15 of 93 Second Class women . . . and 81 of 179 Third Class women. Not to mention the children. Except for Lorraine Allison, all 29 First and Second Class children were saved, but only 23 out of 76 steerage (Third Class) children. Neither the chance to be chivalrous nor the fruits of chivalry seemed to go with a Third Class passage. It was better, but not perfect, in Second Class. Lawrence Beesley remembered an officer stopping two ladies as they started through the gate to First Class. 'May we pass to the boats?' they asked.
'No, madam: your boats are down on your own deck.'

Source: W. Lord, *A Night to Remember*

Last photograph of the *Titanic*

'Room at the Top'   4.3

'There's a girl named Susan Brown,' I said. 'I've taken her out a few times. She's rather attractive.'
'Who is she?'
'Her father owns a factory near Leddersford. He's on the Warley Council.'
She looked at me with a curious pity. 'Money marries money, lad. Be careful she doesn't break your heart. Is she really a nice lass, though?'
'She's lovely,' I said, 'Not just lovely to look at - she's sweet and innocent and good.'
'I bet she doesn't work for a living either, or else does a job for pin money. What good's a girl like that to you? Get one of your own class, lad, go to your own people.'

(Susan's father) 'I'll make you a rich man - a damned sight better off than you'll ever be in local government - on one condition.' He paused; suddenly he looked old and sick. 'Just one condition: you never see Susan again or communicate with her in any way.'

Source: John Braine, *Room at the Top* (1952)

Questions

1. Social class inequalities are shown clearly in data 4.1. Briefly describe these inequalities. Can you think of any other clear-cut class inequalities from Victorian times?

2. The gladiators who killed each other in Roman arenas were slaves (see unit 1 in this section). In the Vietnamese War the front line American troops were usually lower class whites and blacks. Using data 4.2, discuss the view that the value placed on human life is connected to people's positions in the stratification system.

3. Explain the reactions to the young man's relationship with Susan Brown.

Coursework idea

Interview people of your own age and of your grandparents' generation on the subject of social class. Ask them about their feelings and experiences of class. Ask the older generation what changes (if any), they have seen in the class system during their lifetimes.

5 Class divisions

Introduction

In March 1988 Mrs. Thatcher told us, 'In the world we now live, divisions into class are meaningless. We are all working people now'. Sociologists would totally reject this view. Many would argue that social class is *the* most important division in British society.

This unit looks at a range of evidence which supports the sociological view of social class.

5.1

Mrs. Thatcher with multi-millionaire Charles Forte at the official opening of his new motorway services on the M25 in 1987.
This picture includes a
- prime minister
- multi-millionaire
- photographer
- kitchen hand

Infant mortality 5.2

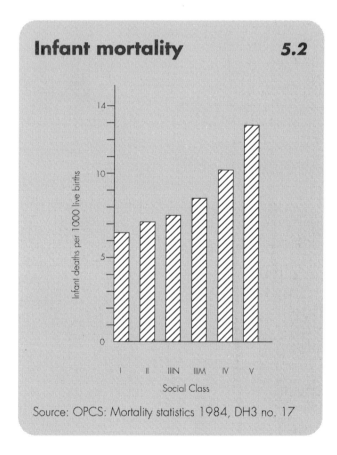

Source: OPCS: Mortality statistics 1984, DH3 no. 17

Social class as defined by the Registrar General 5.3

I Professional -	doctor, accountant, solicitor	**III M Skilled manual -**	bricklayer, printer, electrician
II Intermediate -	manager, engineer, teacher	**IV Semi-skilled manual -**	postman, barman, telephone operator
III N Skilled non-manual -	cashier, clerk, shop assistant	**V unskilled manual -**	kitchen hand, labourer office cleaner

Distribution of wealth 5.4

United Kingdom	Percentages and £ billion			
	1971	1976	1981	1985
Marketable wealth				
Percentage of wealth owned by:				
Most wealthy 1%	31	24	21	20
Most wealthy 5%	52	45	40	40
Most wealthy 10%	65	60	54	54
Most wealthy 25%	86	84	77	76
Most wealthy 50%	97	95	94	93

Source: *Social Trends*, 1989

Distribution of income 5.5

United Kingdom			Percentages			
	Quintile groups of households					
	Bottom fifth	Next fifth	Middle fifth	Next fifth	Top fifth	Total
1976	7.4	12.7	18.0	24.0	37.9	100.0
1981	7.1	12.4	17.9	24.0	38.6	100.0
1985	6.7	11.8	17.4	24.0	40.2	100.0
1986	5.9	11.4	17.0	23.9	41.7	100.0

(After tax has been deducted and state benefits added)

Source: *Social Trends*, 1989

5.6

Round the World by Concorde — FROM £11,850

Orlando • Las Vegas • Hawaii • Fiji • Sydney • Bali • Singapore • Kathmandu • Cairo

Round the World on Concorde - short of flying to the moon, the absolute ultimate in jet set travel, for people who enjoy doing things in style. Your itinerary provides a fascinating series of highlights and contrasts around the globe. An exciting medley of countries and cultures.

Take-off!

The beautiful Pacific

Questions

1. Using information from data 5.1-5.3, discuss Mrs. Thatcher's view that in today's world, 'divisions into social class are meaningless'.

2. a) What percentage of wealth did the most wealthy 1% own in 1985?

   b) What percentage of income did the bottom fifth receive in 1986?

   c) Use the data on the distribution of wealth and income to support the view that social class creates major divisions in UK society.

3. Using data 5.6 as part of your answer, briefly summarise some of the benefits of being at the top of the class system.

Coursework idea

Examine a range of inequalities linked to social class in areas such as health, education, housing, leisure, consumer durables, income and wealth. Publications such as the *General Household Survey* and *Social Trends* will provide useful information.

Introduction

This unit looks at social mobility in the class system. Data 6.1 examines the class background of Queen's Counsels (QCs) who are known as 'silks' because they have the right to wear silk gowns. They are the top barristers in a highly paid profession.

This study confirms the findings of many other studies - to reach the top it is a considerable help to be born at or near the top. There are, however, many exceptions as the information in this unit shows.

The old school tie still makes for a silk future

6.1

**by Jon Craig
Home Affairs
Correspondent**

Dressed in long wigs, breeches and buckled patent shoes, Anthony Thornton and John Hand stood side by side in the Royal Gallery of the House of Lords last week.

They were to be sworn in as Queen's Counsels, a promotion likely to take them to the top of the barristers' earnings league.

But their routes to the top and their social backgrounds are starkly different. Thornton is the son of an army officer and went to Eton and Oxford. Hand grew up in a terraced house in Huddersfield and went to a technical high school and Nottingham University; his father was a lorry driver.

Of the 54 new silks we spoke to only 15 attended state schools - 10 went to grammar schools, four to comprehensives and one to secondary modern. By contrast, 39 went to fee-paying schools - 31 to public schools and eight to direct grant schools.

Moreover, Oxbridge still dominated the new intake, as it does the bar in general: 34 of the 48 graduates had gone to Oxford or Cambridge. Of the 13 non-

John Hand QC: the lorry driver's son is one of 57 new silks

Oxbridge graduates, London and Exeter universities had three each; seven - including two of the three old Etonians - were non-graduates.

Anatomy of the QC

	1978 (%)	1988 (%)
State School	32	28
Fee-paying school	68	72
Oxbridge	68	63
Other universities	24	24
No university	8	13
Women	5.5	7

We also looked at what their fathers did for a living and found

that most still come from the two top social classes, professional and managerial. Six had fathers who were lawyers, there were 10 businessmen, four officers in the armed forces, a surgeon, a priest and a tax inspector.

Hand, the lorry driver's son, now drives a Mercedes, but he says it was a grind to make it into the profession from an ordinary background.

Thornton says that the only reason that the proportion of state school and redbrick university entrants has grown is because the profession has got larger.

But there are many allegations of pro-Oxbridge discrimination. Nigel Baker, a headmaster's son who went to Southampton University, claims some London chambers will consider only Oxbridge graduates.

'Although grammar school people are better represented than they used to be, Oxbridge still has a stranglehold on the prosperous areas of the law and some chambers look no further than Oxford and Cambridge.'

A Newcastle University graduate, Shaun Spencer, a draughtsman's son practising in his home town of Leeds, agrees. 'It's easier for grammar school people to get a start in the provinces, but somebody who has been to Eton and Oxford would probably be better placed to get a start in commercial chambers in London,' he said.

Anthony Giddens, professor of sociology at Cambridge, says most upward mobility in social class is because there are now more jobs in the higher categories and a decline in working-class jobs.

'But,' he said, 'for the son of a lorry driver to become a QC - what we call long-range mobility - is pretty rare.'

Source: *Sunday Times*, 11.4.88
© Times Newspapers Limited 1988

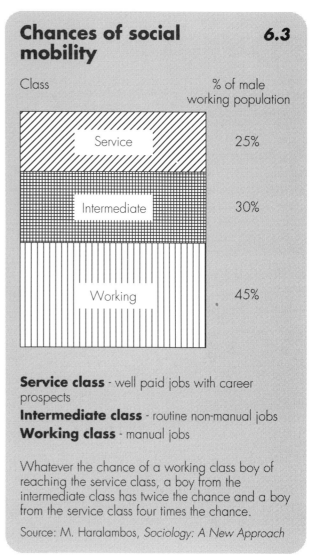

Chances of social mobility

Class   % of male working population

Class	% of male working population
Service	25%
Intermediate	30%
Working	45%

Service class - well paid jobs with career prospects
Intermediate class - routine non-manual jobs
Working class - manual jobs

Whatever the chance of a working class boy of reaching the service class, a boy from the intermediate class has twice the chance and a boy from the service class four times the chance.

Source: M. Haralambos, *Sociology: A New Approach*

Questions

1. According to data 6.1
   a) What is the class background of the majority of Queen's Counsels? Give examples.
   b) What kind of schools did most QCs attend? What does this suggest about their class background?
   c) What is the reason for most upward mobility?
   d) Why is John Hand's career referred to as 'long-range mobility'?

2. The problem with well known examples of upward mobility is that they give the impression that everybody has an equal opportunity. Discuss this statement with reference to data 6.2 and 6.3.

3. The size of the service class has almost doubled in 30 years. What effect might this have on social mobility?

Coursework idea

Interview a sample of adult males in order to investigate social mobility. Find out their present job and their father's last job. Classify these jobs in terms of the Registrar General's (or another) definition of social class. Find out the extent of social mobility and the effect of social class background on social mobility.

Section 6
POVERTY

1 Third World poverty

Introduction

Poverty is a global problem. It is present in every country in the world but is far worse in some than in others. In the Third World (the developing countries of Asia, Africa and Latin America), absolute poverty is widespread.

Absolute poverty means that people are unable to meet basic human needs such as adequate food, clothing and shelter.
This unit looks at some of the reasons for poverty in the Third World.

Two views of poverty 1.1

There are two main explanations for poverty in the Third World. The first sees the Third World as underdeveloped. In time it will catch up to the West as its industry, agriculture and commerce develop. Then, the absolute poverty of today will be a thing of the past.

The second explanation sees the West as a major cause of Third World poverty. The West is seen to exploit or 'rip-off' the Third World making huge profits from its cheap labour. Third World countries are encouraged to produce 'cash-crops' such as peanuts, bananas and pineapples for sale to the West when they cannot adequately feed their own populations. From this point of view the absolute poverty of the Third World shows no sign of disappearing.

Source: adapted from A. Foster-Carter, *The Sociology of Development*

1.2

1.3

'Approximately 1,500 people die each day from lack of nourishment.'

Catholic Fund for Overseas Development

Charity corrupts giver and taker alike and only increases poverty.

Source: Dostoievsky, *The Possessed*

Exploitation?

In 1982 the West gave $33.3 billion as Aid. In return, the Third World gave the West $109 billion as interest payments on international debt and $278 billion in profits from unequal trade.
In 1986 British companies invested £1.1 billion in the Third World. They took out over £2 billion in profits.

Source: Third World First

Live Aid

Questions

1. Read data 1.1. For each of the explanations suggest how the problem of poverty might be solved.

2. Much of the undernourishment in the world is not due to insufficient food but to the way that food is distributed. Comment on this view with reference to data 1.2.

3. What point is being made by the cartoonist in data 1.3?

4. Most people in the West are concerned about a major famine but not about the kind of daily event outlined in data 1.4. Why not?

5. Do you agree with Dostoievsky (1.5)?

6. Is it reasonable to interpret the information in data 1.6 as exploitation?

7. Data 1.7 shows the 1985 Live Aid Concert at Wembley which raised millions of pounds for famine relief in Africa. During the concert, a member of U2 said, 'It should be the job of governments. If they don't do it we should. But we should also tell the government that they should.' Comment on this view.

Coursework idea

Examine the extent and causes of poverty in a Third World country. Ask a geography teacher to help you find the information. Discuss possible solutions to poverty in that country.

2 Poverty in the past

Introduction

This unit aims to give an impression of what it was like to be poor in Britain during the earlier years of this century. The first extract is written by George Orwell. He was a middle class university graduate who found the poverty he saw in the 1930s degrading and offensive.

Northern England, 1930s — 2.1

The train bore me away, through the monstrous scenery of slag-heaps, chimneys, piled scrap-iron, foul canals, paths of cindery mud criss-crossed by the prints of clogs. This was March, but the weather had been horribly cold and everywhere there were mounds of blackened snow. As we moved slowly through the outskirts of the town we passed row after row of little grey slum houses running at right angles to the embankment. At the back of one of the houses a young woman was kneeling on the stones, poking up the leaden waste-pipe which ran from the sink inside and which I suppose was blocked. I had time to see everything about her - her sacking apron, her clumsy clogs, her arms reddened by the cold. She looked up as the train passed, and I was almost near enough to catch her eye. She had a round pale face, the usual exhausted face of the slum girl who is twenty-five and looks forty, thanks to miscarriages and drudgery; and it wore, for the second in which I saw it, the most desolate, hopeless expression I have ever seen. It struck me then that we are mistaken when we say that 'It isn't the same for them as it would be for us,' and that people bred in the slums can imagine nothing but the slums. For what I saw in her face was not the ignorant suffering of an animal. She knew well enough what was happening to her - understood as well as I did how dreadful a destiny it was to be kneeling there in the bitter cold, on the slimy stones of a slum backyard, poking a stick up a foul drain-pipe.

Source: George Orwell, *Road to Wigan Pier*

Escape to Hell — 2.2

My grandfather was 17 when this picture of him and his comrades was taken.
It was the first photograph to graphically illustrate the realities of war in France.
He was an apprentice engineer in Litherland near Liverpool, but money was so low and conditions so bad he followed Lord Kitchener's advice and joined up. (When you've got nothing, you've got nothing to lose!)
The combined result of the gas and the mud was to destroy many of the men both physically and mentally for the rest of their lives.

Source: Peter Rawes (Musician)

Liverpool in the 1930s 2.3

That was the first of many years of nights I spent tossing restlessly, napping, waking, unable to settle because of cold or gnawing hunger. Four of us, still dressed in our underwear, were packed somehow into one bed, and Father, Alan and Brian were to manage in the other bed. Mother stayed on the settee with the baby. For a long time I lay and listened to my parents quarrelling with each other, while the baby whimpered and Fiona, her head against my shoulder, chattered inconsequently in her own uneasy sleep, her doll clasped tightly to her. I fell into a doze, from which I was awakened by Mother calling me in the early morning. I was glad to leave the bed, which smelled of urine, put on my gym-slip and blouse and go to her.

Mother, Avril and I sat almost silent in the icy room. Occasionally, we would feed the baby a little of the remaining milk. We warmed it slightly by putting the bottle next to Mother's skin down the front of her dress, and we wrapped the baby in Mother's coat, which had not got much wetted the previous day. I then tucked our two precious blankets round both mother and child. I longed to get out of the fetid room, even if it was only to stand at the front door, but I was too afraid of my mother in her present state to ask permission to do so. The other children came home for lunch, but there was no lunch, and they departed again for school, cold, hungry and in tears, even brave Alan's lips quivering. Mother, Avril and I, like Father, had neither eaten or drunk.

The afternoon dragged on and the children returned, except for Fiona.

'Fiona's ill,' explained Alan anxiously. 'A teacher is going to bring her home in a little while, when she feels better.'

I suppose my mother was past caring, for she said nothing, but, to the griping hunger pains in my stomach, was added a tightening pain of apprehension for Fiona, the frailest of us all. I tried, however, to be cheerful while I helped the boys off with their coats and then put them on again immediately; because they said they were so cold.

Source: H. Forrester, *Two Pence to Cross the Mersey*

2.4

3. Poverty is offensive and disgraceful in a so-called civilised society. Comment on this statement using data 2.3

4. The picture shown in data 2.4 was taken in London around 1900. What indication does it give that poverty today is different than poverty at the turn of the century?

Questions

1. Read data 2.1
   a) What effect did poverty have on the woman?
   b) Why do some people claim, 'It isn't the same for them as it would be for us'?
   c) Why does Orwell reject this claim?
2. Why did the man in data 2.2 join the army?

Coursework idea

Interview people aged sixty and above about poverty in their youth. Discuss how poverty has changed over the years. Try to find out how they define poverty and how their definition affects the way they see poverty today and in the past.

3 Poverty today

Introduction

Defining and measuring poverty is difficult. Many researchers use the idea of relative poverty. This means that poverty is measured in relation to the living standards of the day. In terms of this view, poverty today is different from poverty in the past because living standards have changed over the years. This unit examines poverty in the 1980s.

Poverty in Manchester   3.1

The North-South divide is irrelevant to the people of Manchester. The divide is the one on their doorstep, between those who can afford to shop in the smart but ugly Arndale Centre and those who resort to the shabby shops in Oldham Street where almost everything is either second-hand or second-rate.

This second, poorer, Manchester was spotlighted in a report published by the city council which found that a third of Manchester's 170,000 households were living in poverty. Instead of using the much criticised method of assessing poverty in terms of the income support (previously supplementary benefit) level, the researchers looked at people's ability to buy 16 goods and services which are generally accepted as basic necessities of life.

Those who were unable to afford three or more of these items, such as beds for everyone in the household, a warm waterproof coat, carpets in the living room and meat or fish every other day, were considered poor.

Thomas Cook, a retired engine driver, does not have, or buy, at least half the goods on the list, making him one of the 9 per cent who are considered to be living in 'intense poverty'. On his pension of £42.79, he can barely afford the dreary cheap shops of Oldham Street, let alone the department stores in the Arndale Centre. The real value of his pension is declining because of cuts in the benefit system.

Meals are usually bacon or hamburgers, clothes are bought second-hand and he has had the same furniture since before he was made redundant 15 years ago. Talking to the residents of the estates of east Manchester about how they manage on welfare benefits, the same words reoccur - the 'catalogue' (of cheap mail order goods paid weekly), the 'market' where the stalls like those in Oldham Street sell the cheap and the shoddy and 'Oxfam', the collective, if inaccurate, name given to all the charity shops. 'Jumbles' are mentioned frequently, too.

It is the pensioners who have the most difficult task coping. Many of the younger people can earn some money moonlighting in casual jobs, but the older people eke out their existence on weekly sums which would buy a modest meal for two in a London restaurant.

Source: adapted from *The Independent*, 9.1.89; Cartoon Child Poverty Action Group

Poverty in London 3.2

In 1985 and 1986, Peter Townsend and a team of researchers investigated poverty in London. Using the Government's own figures they found that the income of the poorest 10% of London households fell by more than 23% between 1983 and 1985. On the basis of one measurement of relative poverty, 1.8 million Londoners are poor. Townsend claims that part of the reason for poverty is inadequate state benefits.

Source: adapted from *The Guardian*, 4.6.87

Spending patterns 3.3

	Family on state benefit	All households
housing repairs	£0.82	£5.89
fuel	£11.46	£12.26
food	£30.50	£45.20
alcohol	£2.47	£8.69
tobacco	£6.59	£4.95
clothing and footwear	£3.55	£16.64
durable household goods	£3.13	£19.56
other goods	£5.69	£16.53
transport	£4.40	£30.46
services	£4.78	£25.04
miscellaneous	£0.45	£1.47

Source: J. Bradshaw and J. Morgan, *New Society*, 6.3.87

3.4

Questions

1. Do you think the method of measuring poverty in data 3.1 is reasonable? Explain your answer.

2. The Welfare State is supposed to provide a 'safety net' to prevent people from falling into poverty.

    a) What point is the cartoonist making in data 3.1?

    b) In view of data 3.1 and 3.2, is the safety net working?

3. Suggest reasons to explain the fall in income of the poorest 10% of households mentioned in data 3.2.

4. What are the main similarities and differences between the spending patterns of the family living on state benefit and all households (3.3)? Why are some spending patterns fairly similar and others very different?

5. Data 3.4 is making a serious point. What is it?

Coursework idea

Draw up a list of 16 goods and services which you think are basic necessities (as in data 3.1). Ask a representative sample of people if they see these items as basic necessities and if they agree that people are poor if they are unable to afford 3 or more items. Discuss with them the reasons for their views. Are there any patterns in your results, eg do older people tend to take one view, young people another?

4 Causes of poverty

Introduction

There are many explanations for poverty. One type of explanation blames the poor - they are work-shy, they waste money, they don't budget properly. Sometimes the Government is singled out for blame for providing inadequate benefits. Another type of explanation blames society as a whole and in particular the capitalist system. It takes the view that the poor are poor because the rich are rich. In other words poverty would cease to be a problem if income and wealth were equally distributed.

'Don't shop when you're hungry'   4.1

SHOPPING ON A BUDGET

1. Shop around - If necessary visit a number of stores and compare prices.
2. Generally groceries are more expensive in small general stores than in chain supermarkets.
3. A supermarket's 'Own Brand' products are usually cheaper (e.g. Fine-Fare Yellow Packs).
4. Some shops reduce goods at or near the 'Sell-By' date, or if the packaging is damaged. These may still be worthwhile buys if used quickly.
5. Remember - Special offers are good but only if you REALLY want the item.
6. Read and compare labels to check prices and amounts.
   eg 400g pack Biscuits @ 28p 7p/100g
       300g pack Biscuits @ 24p 8p/100g
   Don't be deceived by bulky packaging.
7. Use a shopping list and keep to it as far as possible.
8. Don't shop when hungry - You may be tempted to buy more than you need.
9. Tinned or frozen - i.e. convenience foods, tend to be dear. It is cheaper to make your own.
10. Buy fruit and vegetables that are in season - if possible buy at markets or grow your own.
11. It is not necessary to have meat or fish every day - Use cheese or eggs or vegetables, or substitute with soya.
12. Less expensive meats are just as good for you as the more expensive cuts.
13. Try to plan your meals in advance. Base one meal on an earlier one.
14. Wholemeal bread contains more fibre, iron and vitamins than white bread and is only a little more expensive.
15. Watch your spending on sweets, cakes, biscuits, puddings, jams, etc. All these give you little nutritional value.

Source: *National Union Journal*, May 1988

4.2

Source: *National Union Journal*, May 1988

Professor Peter Townsend, who last year completed a study for the Low Pay Unit based on the Family Expenditure Survey (produced by the Department of Employment), calculates that the real income of the bottom ten per cent fell by 5.5 per cent between 1983 and 1985 and estimates a similar drop between 1981 and 1985. Only a week before the DHSS statistics were published, a parliamentary question produced the following from the DE: from 1983 to 1986, the poorest ten per cent of single pensioners saw their disposable income increase by two per cent less than inflation; for the same period, the poorest ten per cent of married couples with two children saw their disposable income rise by four per cent less than inflation.

Source: *The Guardian*

4.3

Homeless youth begs for money, London 1989

Who's to blame?   4.4

Owen continued, 'The theory that drunkenness, laziness and inefficiency are the causes of poverty are so many devices fostered by those who are selfishly interested in maintaining the present state of affairs for the purpose of preventing us from discovering the real cause of our present condition.'
'Well what do you reckon is the cause of poverty,' demanded Easton.
'The present system of Capitalism,' retorted Owen. 'It is not the poor themselves who are at fault but the way that wealth is divided. All the people in the working class are suffering and starving and fighting in order that the rich people, the capitalist class, can live in luxury and do nothing. These are the wretches that cause poverty. They produce nothing but exist on the work done by the people.'
'It can't never be altered,' interrupted old Linden. 'I don't see no sense in all this 'ere talk. There's always been rich and poor in the world and there always will be.'
'But that's where you're wrong,' shouted Owen. 'We can change all that. The rich are only rich because they rob the poor. They have got control of the land, the machinery, the tools and use that control to exploit us. We work all our lives and instead of being paid the real value of our work we are paid a pittance. The Capitalist class keeps the rest as their profit and try to persuade us that it is rightfully theirs. But they have not worked for it - they have just sat and watched us. But we can change all that. If all the working men were to unite we would be too strong for them and they would be forced to give us what is rightfully ours. No one would own the land, the mines, the factories, they would belong to the whole community. We would all work and in return receive a just wage which would permit everyone to live a civilised life. Then there would be no poverty.'
The men started to shift uncomfortably and one or two of them on the edge of the group started to collect up their tools ready for the afternoon's labour.

Source: Robert Tressell, *The Ragged Trousered Philanthropists*

Questions

1. Read data 4.1 which contains advice to people on state benefits.
   a) Do you consider the advice reasonable?
   b) Do you think poverty would be reduced if people followed this and similar advice?
2. Judging from data 4.2 what do you think the cartoonist feels about advising the poor to be careful with their money?
3. Data 4.3 can be used to argue that poverty in the 1980s is due, at least partly, to inadequate state benefits. Use the data to make this point.
4. Do you agree with Owen or with Linden (4.4) or with neither? Give reasons for your answer.

Coursework idea

Read the chapters on poverty in Sociology textbooks. Make a list of the causes of poverty. Interview a representative sample asking people for their views on the causes of poverty. Then ask them for their comments on the list of causes you have made. Analyse the responses for patterns, eg do young people tend to see different causes than older people?

RACE AND ETHNICITY

1 Explanations for racism

Introduction

Racial prejudice is the belief that,
1) the human species is divided into races,
2) some races are superior to others,
3) members of different races should be treated differently,
4) all members of a particular race share the same characteristics.

Racial discrimination means acting out racial prejudice - treating members of other racial groups as inferior and treating them in terms of a racial stereotype.

Racism is the term used to cover both racial prejudice and discrimination. This unit looks at explanations for racism.

Justifications for racism   *1.1*

We created civilisation

We are nearer to God

We are more intelligent

We gave you religion and education

The stranger   *1.2*

First Polite Native: "Who's 'im, Bill?"
Second ditto: "A stranger!"
First ditto: "'Eave 'arf a brick at 'im!"

Source: *Punch*, 1854

Ancient Rome   *1.3*

If the Tiber floods, or the Nile fails to flood, if the sky is darkened, if the earth trembles, if famine war or plague occurs, then immediately one shout went up:
'The Christians to the Lions!'

Source: James Mitchell (ed), *Man in Society*

Human rights   *1.4*

Article 1
All human beings are born free and equal in dignity and rights.

Article 2
Everyone is entitled to all the rights and freedoms set forth in this Declaration, without distinction of any kind, such as race, colour, sex, language, religion, political or other opinion, national or social origin, property, birth or other status.

Source: United Nations, *Universal Declaration of Human Rights*, 1948

Questions

1. From one point of view racism exists to justify oppression, exploitation and mistreatment.

   a) Look at data 1.1 and outline the ways in which whites have justified the conquest and oppression of non-whites.

   b) These justifications are based on 'myths'. Explain this statement.

2. Explain the behaviour of 'the natives' in data 1.2. How can their attitude help to provide an explanation for racism?

3. We often blame our own problems on others. Why? Use your answer to explain the behaviour of the Romans in data 1.3. How can the attitude of the Romans help to provide an explanation for racism?

4. Data 1.4 is a totally anti-racist statement. Briefly explain why.

Coursework idea

Study a group which has suffered from oppression, eg Africans during the era of slavery or Jews in Nazi Germany. Look at the ways in which their oppression was justified. To what extent do theories of racism explain the treatment of the group you have chosen to study?

2 Racism in children's books

Introduction

We learn to be racist - it doesn't come naturally. Our prejudices, stereotypes and ideas about different ethnic groups and societies are learned from our family, friends, school and the mass media. Studies have shown that many children learn racial stereotypes at an early age. Today, most publishers, particularly those who publish children's books, try to avoid racism. However, as this unit shows, children's books in the past told a different story.

The Story of Little Black Sambo   2.1

ONCE upon a time there was a little black boy, and his name was Little Black Sambo.

And his Mother was called Black Mumbo.

Source: Helen Bannerman, *The Story of Little Black Sambo* (first published in 1899)

The story of Dr. Dolittle   2.2

Well, that night Prince Bumpo came secretly to the Doctor in prison and said to him: 'White Man, I am an unhappy prince. Years ago I went in search of the Sleeping Beauty, whom I had read of in a book. And having travelled through the world many days, I at last found her and kissed the lady very gently to awaken her - as the book said I should. 'Tis true indeed that she awoke. But when she saw my face she cried out, "Oh, he's black!" And she ran away and wouldn't marry me - but went to sleep again somewhere else. So I came back, full of sadness, to my father's kingdom.

Now I hear that you are a wonderful magician and have many powerful potions. So I come to you for help. If you will turn me white, so that I may go back to the Sleeping Beauty, I will give you half my kingdom and anything besides you ask.'
'Prince Bumpo,' said the Doctor, looking thoughtfully at the bottles in his medicine-bag, 'supposing I made your hair a nice blonde colour - would not that do instead to make you happy?'
'No', said Bumpo. 'Nothing else will satisfy me. I must be a white prince.'

Source: Hugh Lofting, *The Story of Dr. Dolittle* (first published in 1922)

Noddy 2.3

Noddy wriggled and shouted and wailed

Source: Enid Blyton, *Here Comes Noddy Again* (first published in 1951)

Coursework idea

Compare how ethnic minorities are portrayed in children's books from the 1980s and in children's books from earlier years of this century. Try to explain any differences you find.

'The native end of town' 2.4

'Where is this jail or whatever it is?'
'In the middle of the town; at the corner of the Cathedral and the Stretta Fontana. You can't mistake the street because there's a double row of palms on either side. I dropped one of the policemen a couple of dollars and he told me they're keeping him there until tomorrow, as da Silva wants to talk to him. Then , unless he tells the Mayor something he wants to know, they are going to take him to the proper jail in the native end of the town. If they ever get him in there, you'll never see him again. It's full of Indians, niggers, and half-breeds, the scum of the earth. If you want to see him alive again you'll have to get him out tonight.'

Source: W.E. Johns, *Cruise of the Condor* (first published 1933)

Questions

1. *The Story of Little Black Sambo* (2.1) used to be seen as a harmless story for young children. Today many people see it as racist. Which view do you take? Give reasons for your answer.

2. If you were a librarian, would you buy copies of *The Story of Dr Dolittle* (2.2) for the children's section of your library? Explain your answer.

3. Data 2.3 shows Noddy being attacked by wicked golliwogs. Is this a racist picture? Give reasons for your answer.

4. According to data 2.1 - 2.4, what is a black person like?

5. Racism in children's books is particularly serious. Explain this statement using what you know about the importance of socialisation in the early years of childhood.

3 Welcome to Britain?

Introduction

In Britain after World War 2 (1939-1945), there were large numbers of vacancies for jobs in factories, the National Health Service, transport and other services. In 1948 the Government passed a Nationality Act making all colonial and Commonwealth citizens British and advertised for them to fill the job vacancies.

Concern about the effects of what many saw as a 'flood of immigrants' grew. The welcome turned sour. The Government passed a series of Acts from 1962 to 1981 restricting immigration to Britain.

The invitation 3.1

Source: Institute of Race Relations, *How Racism Came To Britain*

The concern 3.2

'. . . by the end of the century there would be four million people of the New Commonwealth or Pakistan here.
Now that is an awful lot and I think it means that people are really rather afraid that this country might be rather swamped by people with a different culture and, you know, the British character has done so much for democracy, for law, and done so much throughout the world that if there is any fear that it might be swamped people are going to react and be rather hostile to those coming in.'

Source: Margaret Thatcher, January, 1978

The Prophecy   3.3

OTHERS WERE LESS POLITE AND, PRETENDING TO SPEAK FOR THE COMMON PEOPLE, STOKED THEIR RACIST FEARS AND FANTASIES.

'As I look ahead, I am filled with foreboding. Like the Roman, I seem to see the River Tiber foaming with much blood.'

Enoch Powell. 1968.

Source: Institute of Race Relations, *How Racism Came To Britain*

The facts   3.4

In 1986, 4.5 per cent of the population belonged to ethnic minority groups, with two-thirds coming from the West Indies and Guyana or Pakistan, India and Bangladesh. The proportion of the population belonging to ethnic minorities will continue to rise over the next few years because of their younger profile.

Just over 7 per cent of the 747,800 live births in 1987 were to mothers born in the New Commonwealth and Pakistan, but this is becoming a less reliable guide to the number of non-white births since many non-white babies now have mothers born here.

The ethnic minority groups continue to have markedly different age structures: 21 per cent of whites are aged 60 or over, compared with 6 per cent of the West Indian/Guyanese ethnic group. The flow of immigrants and emigrants almost balances itself. While 219,600 immigrants arrived in the five years to the end of 1987, 189,200 left, leaving a net inflow of 30,400, compared with a net outflow of 20,500 in the previous five years. But while the inflow from the Commonwealth remained the same in these two periods, the numbers from the EC increased from 29,200 to 51,900, attracted by the right to work.

Source: *The Independent*

The headlines   3.5

'Asian flood swamps airport'   (Express)
'3,000 Asians flood Britain'   (Sun)
'2,000 Indians smuggled in   (Express)

Source: Paul Trowler, *Investigating the Media*

𝒬uestions

1. According to data 3.1, what kinds of jobs were available to immigrants?

2. Mrs. Thatcher (3.2) is mainly concerned about non-white immigration (the New Commonwealth consists of all Commonwealth countries except Canada, Australia and New Zealand).

   a) Do you share her concern? Give reasons for your answer.

   b) Some have seen her views as racist though she strongly denies this. What is your opinion of her speech? Explain your answer.

3. In 1968 Enoch Powell MP (3.3) prophesied that non-white immigration would lead to 'rivers of blood' on the streets of Britain. Do you agree with the comment in d ita 3.3 that he 'stoked racist fears and fantasies'?

4. Read data 3.4. Does it support the fear voiced by Margaret Thatcher that Britain will be 'swamped by people with a different culture'?

5. Headlines such as those in data 3.5 have been described as 'irresponsible' and 'inflammatory'. Comment on this view.

Coursework idea

Interview a representative sample of people about their views on immigration. After obtaining their views, present them with the facts (3.4 and further material from *Social Trends*). How close are their views to the facts? Do they change their views when presented with the facts?

4 Racism in Britain

Introduction

A number of studies have shown that racism is widespread in Britain. This unit examines some of the evidence for racism - in employment, education, the police and the criminal system.

It shows the extremes of racism in Britain - the National Front and racist attacks. It ends with a view of what it feels like to be black and living in the 'Motherland'.

On arrival in the 1950s . . .   4.1

THEY WERE PAID LESS FOR THE SAME WORK:

HOURS: 40
FOUNDRY WORK:
AGE: 30
YEARS OF SERVICE: 8

HOURS 40
FOUNDRY WORK:
AGE: 30
YEARS OF SERVICE: 8

THEY WERE ASKED TO WORK LONGER HOURS:

THEY WERE DENIED PROMOTION AND ASKED TO WORK BELOW THEIR QUALIFICATIONS . . . .

Well, this puts my Philosophy Degree to the test....

Source: Institute of Race Relations, *How Racism Came To Britain*

Stephen Anderson: assault claims

In 1989 . . .   4.2

The Ministry of Defence has commissioned an urgent study into the attitudes of ethnic minorities to the armed forces because of growing concern about the shortage of recruits.

Last year only 1.6% of all applications came from ethnic minorities, although they accounted for 5.7% of the population in the 15-24 age bracket.

Fear of racial abuse is one factor. The publicity given to cases such as Stephen Anderson a private in the Devon and Dorset regiment who is suing the army under the Race Relations Act has persuaded many potential recruits that the army is a hot-bed of racism.

Anderson the only black member of his regiment alleged that he was beaten up, had his life threatened, and was called 'nigger' and 'coon'.

Source: *Sunday Times*, 19.2.89

You learn quickly though

On the plane over I got chatting to a woman who I found out was a nurse over here . . . She asked me whether I was going to be a pupil nurse or a student nurse. Well, I hadn't registered any difference at the time. Then she explained that SEN pupils were lower than SRN students and that Trinidad didn't even recognise the SEN qualification. She told me I could change when I got here, since I'd passed the General Nursing Council exam at home . . . She did drum it in that I should tell them I wanted to change as soon as I got here . . . I went to the Matron and demanded to change. They were taken aback but there was nothing they could do about it because I'd passed the test. I didn't realise then that they thought if you were Black you were stupid. You learn quickly though.

Source: Sallie Westwood, 'Race, Gender and Work', *Social Studies Review*, March 1988

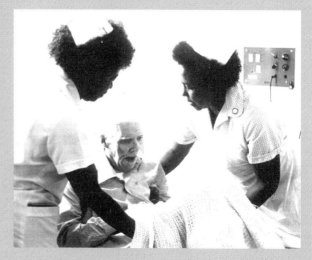

Black nurses face many barriers at every stage of their careers

Education - The Swann Report

In 1985 the report of the Swann Committee, which was appointed by the government to study ethnic minority education, was published. The report stated that some teachers tended to see pupils in terms of their skin colour. In one school, some of the teachers regularly made racist remarks like sending black students 'back to the chocolate factory'. They were 'amazed' when they discovered that many black students were bright - 'My goodness he's bright, where does he get it from'. Staffroom gossip sometimes labelled blacks as troublemakers which meant that teachers jumped to conclusions before even meeting students.

The following extract from a conversation between a researcher and eight black students shows their anger and resentment at the attitudes of some teachers.

Michael: 'It's like once the man (referring to the teacher) come in the class, and ask me in front of the class, 'Why me coffee coloured', he say, 'How come Wallace dark, and Kennedy black and Kevin a bit browner? How come you that, you a half-breed? . . .' That's how he is, he just come around, crack him few sarcastic jokes about black kids.'

Source: adapted from *The Times Educational Supplement* 25.10.85

Paul: 'But they're not nice at all. They're not nice. The jokes aren't nice. The jokes are disrespectful.'
Kevin: 'They're not jokes man . . . What he is doing is running you down. He's just bringing you down like dirt. Nobody is bring me down (said with anger). Every time I'm chuck out of (subject) completely man, because every time in (subject) he always keep calling me something about me colour and I answer back.'
Errol: 'The teachers are forever picking on the black boys.'
'The boys said this 'hassle' affected their academic performance because, in the words of one, . . .
'We got no time, as you sit down to work they pin something on you.'
Students reacted to this treatment by forming their own 'all-black' group which was anti-school and to some extent, anti-white. They moved round the school together and spoke in patois (Caribbean dialect) to assert their blackness. Asked to explain their behaviour, one member of the group said:
'. . .We try to get our own back on them. We behave ignorantly towards them, and when the teachers talk to us and tell us to do something we don't do it, because we just think about how they treated us.'

Police prejudice 4.5

In 1984 the findings of an independent study of London's police force were revealed. The study was carried out by the Policy Studies Institute and was commissioned by the police itself.

It found that there was evidence of racial prejudice among policemen of all ranks, that the police sometimes used racist language and there was racist graffitti in some police toilets. The presence of a small number of black or Asian police officers had little effect on the level of racist talk, and police often showed ignorance of the ethnic groups living in their areas - for instance confusing Indian with Pakistani. Officers claim that their attitudes do not affect the way they do their job but the study concludes that there is evidence of some inferior treatment of black and Asian people by the police, for example:

- black people are more likely to be stopped by the police than white
- the police tend to connect crime wth black people
- the police are reluctant to act against racist attackers

Source: Vivien Thom, *Prejudice*

'When we come to power, all black people will be sent out of the country back to where they came from. No matter how long or how many generations they have been in our country, they will be repatriated.'

Source: John Tyndall (1976), Chairman of the National Front

In prison 4.6

Young black offenders are more likely to be prosecuted than white juveniles for similar offences, according to a report published today. The National Association for the Care and Resettlement of Offenders says that sentenced black prisoners have fewer previous convictions than white prisoners punished for the same type of offence, and are significantly less likely to have been granted bail.

The association's report shows that 14 per cent of prisoners in England and Wales are from ethnic minorities, more than twice the proportion in the general population.

Entitled *Some Facts and Findings about Black People in the Criminal Justice System*, it states that of the 50,270 people in prison on 30 June last year, 7,050 (14 per cent) were from ethnic minorities, compared with 6,000 (12.5 per cent) two years earlier.

The organisation's director, Vivien Stern, said: "These figures do not show that black people are more prone to crime than white people, but they do suggest that black people who offend are more likely to go to prison."

She urged higher priority for race relations training for magistrates and court staff, and efforts to recruit more black judges, magistrates, court clerks, probation officers and prison staff.

The National Front 4.7

National Front Rally, London, 1980

50 times more at risk   4.8

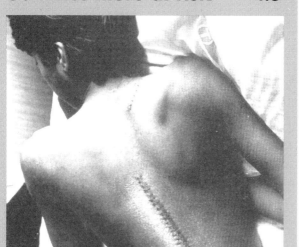

Scotland the brave?   4.9

Until 2 or 3 years ago Scotland which has few Afro-Caribbeans made great play of the idea that it was virtually free of the English disease of race hatred. But a recent survey by the Scottish Council for Racial Equality shows that more than 80% of Pakistanis and Indians have experienced racial abuse, with 58% of Indians registering a physical attack.

These include a particularly violent series of attacks on traders and residents around Glasgow Rangers Ibrox Stadium - in one instance employing hatchets, in another hammer blows to the head and a third, knives and iron bars. Among other targets has been the Scottish Asian Action Committee whose offices have been daubed with swastikas.

Source: *The Guardian*, 13.4.88

Isolated and unwanted   4.10

As a West Indian woman in this country I feel isolated and unwanted . . . The feeling doesn't get any worse it's just there. You know you're not wanted and you just act accordingly, keep yourself to yourself.

Source: Elyse Dodgson, *The Motherland*

6. White, male, lower working class youths are largely responsible for racial attacks (4.8, 4.9). Can you suggest why?
7. Briefly explain Elyse Dodgson's feelings (4.10) using data from this unit.

Questions

1. Briefly outline the evidence for racial discrimination in employment from data 4.1 to 4.3.
2. Using data 4.4 explain how racism can reduce the educational attainment of black students.
3. Racism within an organisation such as the police (4.5) is particularly serious. Why?
4. Why does Vivien Stern (4.6) argue that magistrates need training in race relations?
5. The National Front's demands (4.7) are seen by many people as unrealistic, unfair and just plain stupid. Do you agree? Give reasons for your answer.

Coursework idea

Write to the Commission for Racial Equality for details of cases brought under the Race Relations Act. Summarise a number of these. Show them to a sample of people and ask whether or not they agree with the verdicts and why. Use the information to discuss views on ethnicity and equal opportunity.

Try to explain differences in the responses you get, eg does the age, gender, ethnicity, social class etc of members of your sample affect their responses.

5 On the bright side

Introduction

The previous units have concentrated on the problems faced by ethnic minorities in Britain. This unit looks on the brighter side - to the achievements of blacks and Asians in business, the professions, politics, sport and the mass media. It shows that it is possible for individuals to break through the barriers of racial discrimination.

The unit also looks at one of the steps taken by local authorities to try to ensure equal opportunities for ethnic minorities.

John Barnes

Role models   5.1

To Keith Davidson, Jamaican-born headmaster of the predominantly black, independent John Loughborough School in Tottenham, London, the success of people such as Bruno and Campbell, provides important lessons for his pupils. 'The key thing is that these are black people who have been successful. This is helpful, but we want to get our children to realise that they can be successful in other areas of life as well. They need to see more people from ethnic minorities in areas of responsibility: whether it be education, business, politics. Knowing that blacks need not be relegated to menial roles gives the children motivation to aspire to higher levels.'

Increasingly, such role-models *are* available to black children. Some are highly visible: newscasters such as the BBC's Moira Stuart, and Trevor McDonald on Channel Four, and the three black MPs - Diane Abbott, Bernie Grant and Paul Boateng. There is a black bishop in Croydon - Wilfred Wood - a society of black lawyers and many black business people. In February, two young women were feted, one as Corporate Black Businesswoman of the Year (Yvonne Richardson, a sales manager with Readers Digest) and another as Black Businesswoman of the Year (Jenni Francis who has her own PR company).

According to Francis, black people are proud when one of their own achieves celebrity status, but they find their real role-models closer to home. 'You feel pride that people like Lenny Henry and John Barnes have come through, but it reinforces a belief that was always there. We have always had people to look up to. We pay tribute to our parents who had the get-up-and-go to come over here.'

Another successful young black woman, Marina Salandy-Browne, a BBC Radio 4 producer, stresses that there is already a network of high-achieving blacks in Britain - an emerging middle-class which the white community has not noticed: 'There are a lot of black people driving around in BMWs - and they are not muggers or drug-runners, but people running successful businesses and advertising agencies. There are doctors, engineers and headmistresses. And their success tells young blacks that there are no areas of work that are completely closed.'

Source: *Sunday Times,* 5.3.89
© Times Newspapers Limited 1989

200 millionaires   5.2

Twenty years ago Enoch Powell predicted that immigration would lead to 'rivers of blood' in Britain's streets.

Instead they are paved with gold for some black and Asian settlers, it emerged last night.

Home Secretary Douglas Hurd announced that 200 millionaires have sprung from the ethnic minorities.

And thousands of other immigrants, from the Indian cornershop owner to the factory boss, are generating wealth for the nation.

Mr. Hurd denounced Mr. Powell's 1968 warnings of bloody clashes between white and black communities.

He urged the country never to be complacent about race relations but added: 'As I look forward I am filled with hope. Of course, tensions, resentments, private acts of discrimination continue but, I believe, less virulently than before.'

Notable

'New Commonwealth immigrants and their British-born children and grandchildren have found an accepted place in this country. They are making an increasingly notable contribution to many aspects of British life.'

Mr. Hurd said he looked forward to the day when black Tory MPs joined the four coloured Labour backbenchers elected last year.

Labour deputy leader Roy Hattersley, also speaking in Birmingham, said, the 2.5 million immigrants of the past 20 years had 'proved the false prophets wrong.'

He added: 'A multi-racial society, through its diversity, can add to the richness of the whole community.'

Source: Today, 23.4.88

Equal opportunity   5.3

Lancashire County Council as an equal opportunity employer intends that no job applicant or employee shall receive less favourable treatment because of his or her sex, marital status, race, colour, nationality, national origin, ethnic origin, sexual orientation, or disability, nor be disadvantaged by any other condition or requirement which cannot be shown to be justifiable.

समानता का पक्ष करने वाला एम्पलायर

HINDI

नीति विषयक जन जाहेरात

GUJERATI

प्रसात अफ्रिका द्वारा टिम्पलाइंद

PUNJABI

Note: Other Asian languages are included on this leaflet.

Source: Lancashire County Council

Questions

1. Why are role models (5.1) important for young members of ethnic minority groups?

2. The most visible role models are usually sportspeople such as the footballer John Barnes and the boxer Frank Bruno. This can lead to stereotypes. Discuss this view.

3. It is unusual to find newspaper articles like data 5.2. How are ethnic minorities usually portrayed in the media?

4. Comment on Roy Hattersley's statement (5.2).

5. Lancashire County Council are to be applauded for the statement in data 5.3. Do you agree? Give reasons for your answer.

Coursework idea

Find examples of the achievements of members of ethnic minority groups. Suggest how they can act as role models. Discuss the problems that might arise with stereotypes, particularly with reference to the mass media (see question 2).

Section 8
POLITICS

1 Democracy and totalitarianism

Introduction

The word democracy comes from two Greek words meaning 'people power'. Democracy is generally seen as a system of government in which people have a say in the way they are governed.

Totalitarianism is a form of government in which power is concentrated in the hands of an individual or the state. The mass of the population has little or no say in the way it is governed.

This unit looks at examples of democratic and totalitarian government.

Democracy in Greece   1.1

Pericles

Our government is an original one, modelled on none of our neighbours; indeed others have copied us, but we have copied nobody. We are called a democracy because the whole people and not a minority rule; in the law courts everyone is equal before the law. We appoint our public officials with reference to their merit or ability and not to their family background. No one, not even if he is poverty-stricken, is kept out of politics if he has something to contribute.

Source: Pericles, leader of Athens

BUT

In ancient Greece large sections of the population - slaves, women and children - were not regarded as 'qualified citizens' and therefore not allowed to participate in government.

Source: D. Roberts, *Politics: A New Approach*

Totalitarianism in Germany   1.2

Adolf Hitler, 1935

By 1933 the Nazis were the largest single party in the Reichstag (the German Parliament) and Hitler had become Chancellor of Germany. Hitler got the Reichstag to pass an Enabling Law which enabled him to make laws without the Reichstag having to agree to them. He banned trade unions and political parties other than the Nazi Party. Newspapers and school textbooks were censored. When Hitler became Chancellor in 1933 there were 6 million unemployed. By 1939 Germany was short of workers. During these years the Nazis provided better welfare services, cheap houses and even cheap holidays abroad.

Source: adapted from J.F. Aylett, *Hitler's Germany*

'Political Alphabet' by George Cruikshank

D is a
DESPOT, in
whom ye
may see
A symbol of
all who hate
the word –
FREE

Q stands for
QUESTION –
How long shall
this be
A portrait of
MAN – destin'd
to be free?

Representative democracy

What are the main ideas associated with representative democracies? A government must arise out of public opinion and be answerable to the public. This means a government taking account of the wishes of the people and publicly explaining and justifying its actions. It also means that the people have opportunities to change the government by choosing an alternative. This would require regular elections and a system of checks to prevent one group of people from having too much power. Power concentrated in the hands of one group or a single person can lead to a denial of other features expected in a democracy. For example, it is often thought that governments should act for the benefit of the nation as a whole and not in the interests of a particular group or class. There should be tolerance towards

minority groups. Free speech and a free press should exist. People should have the freedom to meet together when and with whom they wish.

To guarantee these freedoms it is necessary to have an independent system of law courts free from government interference. To prevent the concentration of power, the main functions of government should be divided and each function should be controlled by different groups of people. This would mean that the functions of making laws, carrying out the law and deciding if and when the law has been broken, should not all be the responsibility of the same people.

Source: adapted from A. Renwick and I. Swinburn, Basic Political Concepts

Questions

1. Judged from today's standards, was ancient Greece a democratic society (1.1)?

2. a) Judging from data 1.2, was Nazi Germany a totalitarian society?

   b) Even dictators can receive the support of many of their subjects. With reference to data 1.2, briefly suggest why.

3. The cartoons illustrate acts which are against democracy. Briefly explain why.

4. Which of the aspects of a representative democracy (1.4) were absent in Hitler's Germany (1.3)?

Coursework idea

Charter 88 is an organisation which seeks, among other things, to extend democratic rights in Britain. Write to Charter 88 for a summary of its aims.

In terms of its view of democracy, do you consider Britain to be a democratic society?

2 Democracy in Britain

Introduction

Democracy in Western industrial societies is usually seen to involve universal adult suffrage - the right of all adults to vote in local and national elections. However, as the case of Britain shows, this is a recent development. This unit examines the extension of the franchise (the right to vote) in Britain.

Extension of the franchise 2.1

For centuries the House of Commons was elected by a small minority of the population, mostly wealthy land and property owners. The Great Reform Act of 1832 extended the franchise, or right to vote, to male owners or tenants of property with a rentable value of £10 a year or more. This was a large sum of money - a year's wage for a cook or a maid. It meant that only the middle class received the vote.

In 1867 urban working class males who paid at least £10 a year in rent received the vote and this was extended to rural areas in 1884.

Women had to wait until 1918 before obtaining the vote and then they had to be over 30 years of age. Only in 1928 did they receive the franchise on the same basis as men.

Source: adapted in part from K. Marder, *Parliament and its Work*

The growth of the electorate 2.2

Year	%	Description
Before 1832	3	Franchise generally restricted to owners of land and property
1832	5	£10 householder qualification - enfranchised middle class (male)
1867	9	£10 lodger qualification in boroughs - enfranchised urban working class (male)
1884	16	Borough qualifications extended to counties - enfranchised agricultural workers
1918	47	All men over 21 years and women over 30 years
1928	65	All men and women over 21 years
1969	71	Age qualification reduced to 18 years

Electorate as percentage of total population

Source: D. Roberts, *Politics: A New Approach*

2.3

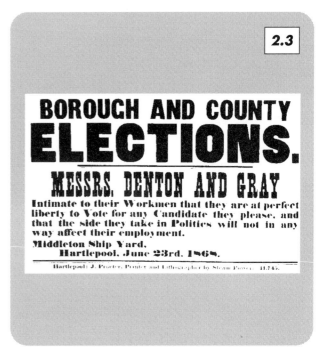

BOROUGH AND COUNTY

ELECTIONS.

MESSRS. DENTON AND GRAY

Intimate to their Workmen that they are at perfect liberty to Vote for any Candidate they please, and that the side they take in Politics will not in any way affect their employment.

Middleton Ship Yard,
Hartlepool, June 23rd, 1868.

Hartlepool: J. Procter, Printer and Lithographer by Steam Power.   11,745.

AN "UGLY RUSH!"

Source: *Punch*, 1870

THE DIGNITY OF THE FRANCHISE

Qualified Voter: "Ah, you may pay rates an' taxes, an' you may 'ave responserbilities an' all; but when it comes to votin', you must leave it to *us men!*"

Source: *Punch*, 1905

Girls Own Paper, 1896   2.6

- 'It is not at all clear that the great majority of women who would obtain the franchise would care to use it. There seems to be no general and wide demand for it. If women want the franchise they will have to ask for it.'
- 'Probably not ten per cent of the female voters would on a purely political question go to the poll.'
- 'The truth is that the intelligence of highly intelligent women is not political. Only a few will take interest in politics steadily and continuously.'
- 'The factory-girl class will be by far the most important class of women voters. The married woman who has no separate house property will have no vote. Political power in many large cities would be chiefly in the hands of young, ill-educated, giddy, and often ill-conducted girls, living in lodgings.'

Questions

1. Provide an explanation for why some received the vote before others (2.1 and 2.2). Refer to power, wealth, income, gender and age in your answer.

2. Why do you think the employers in data 2.3 issued this notice for their workers?

3. Look at cartoons 2.4 and 2.5. What points are the cartoonists making?

4. Data 2.6 was written by Frederick Ryland. It reflects the attitudes of many males of his day. Do you think it reflects any of the stereotypes of women which exist today? Explain your answer.

Coursework idea

Interview a representative sample of people about their views on voting in national elections. You might consider the following questions:

a) Should the franchise be extended further?

b) Should it be illegal not to vote?

c) Should there be regular referenda on important issues?

3 Pressure groups

Introduction

A political party seeks to form a government. It claims to represent the nation as a whole. However, there are many groups in society with their own particular concerns and interests. It is often claimed that for a society to be democratic, these particular or 'sectional' interests must be represented. One of the ways this is done is by means of pressure or interest groups.

This unit examines the role of pressure groups in a democratic society.

Pressure groups   3.1

But just what is a pressure group? The Automobile Association (AA) and the Campaign for Real Ale (CAMRA) are both genuine pressure groups. The AA does not just look after members' interests but acts as a spokesman for the motorist, while CAMRA has successfully campaigned 'to preserve and promote traditional beer'. Many pubs have responded to the challenge. Other groups range from the Royal Commonwealth Society for the Blind to the National Traction Engine Club; from the National Playing Fields Association (which aims to provide and improve play and recreational facilities, especially for the young) to Australia's Limbless Soldiers' Association. Pressure groups set out to influence and affect the way the country is governed. They do not aim to take over the government, even though some of their members may be in Parliament - as trade unionists, lawyers or farmers, for example. Members of pressure groups constantly strive to change government policy by influencing MPs, senior civil servants, businessmen, and leaders of opinion, like newspaper editors. They try to influence public opinion in the hope that the public will directly or indirectly let their views be known to those who rule or wish to rule the nation.

Source: R. May, *Pressure Groups*

Greenpeace advert   3.2

GREENPEACE

MARINE POLLUTION

Pollution in our seas and estuaries is destroying habitats and killing marine life.

Urgent action is needed now to stop the discharge of industrial, chemical and radioactive wastes and the dumping of sewage sludge. The UK and Ireland are the only countries still dumping sewage sludge into the North and Irish seas.

Greenpeace has blocked chemical discharge pipes, confronted dump ships and researched and reported on the effects of toxic pollution.

In 1989, Greenpeace will continue to confront the polluters and to campaign for laws to be amended and enforced to protect our seas.

THANK GOD SOMEONE'S MAKING WAVES

3.3

STOP THE SUFFERING

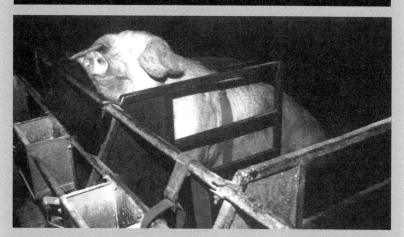

© Helen Cruddas

Today some 400,000 sows spend their lives confined individually in narrow stalls or tethered in rows by girth straps shackled to the floor as is the sow in the above photograph.

This close confinement causes sows severe distress. Consider the scientific account of the reaction of the sow when she is tethered for the first time:

"Following a brief and gentle tug on the tether chain, the sows threw themselves violently backwards, straining against the tether.... Sows thrashed their heads about as they twisted and turned in their struggle to free themselves. Often loud screams were emitted and occasionally individuals crashed bodily against the side bars of the tether stall. This sometimes resulted in the sows collapsing to the floor."

FACTS

1) Immediately after tethering, sows make strenuous efforts to escape. The only explanation that seems to account for this is that the experience is strongly aversive to the sows.

2) In the majority of cases bedding is not provided and the sows stand or lie on concrete. They are unable to exercise their limbs or turn round and in advanced pregnancy have difficulty in getting up and lying down comfortably. Lameness, sores and hip problems are common as is stereotyped behaviour such as bar gnawing.

3) These systems have been condemned by report after report: by parliamentary committees; by scientists; by the government's own Codes of Recommendations for the Welfare of Pigs.

4) The European Parliament voted on 20th February, 1987 for these systems to be discontinued throughout the EEC. The European Parliament, however, has only an advisory role and it is up to governments to act.

5) The time has come for the UK Government to announce the phasing-out of both dry sow stalls and tether stalls within 5 years.

Source: Compassion in World Farming

WHAT YOU CAN DO

1) Send for a copy of our National Petition and collect as many signatures as you can.

2) Send an s.a.e. for 20 copies of this leaflet to distribute to your friends, neighbours and colleagues.

3) Ask your local butcher/supermarket to ensure that meat is labelled with method of production, i.e. "factory farm" or "welfare meat" as is produced by The Real Meat Company.

4) Ask your MP to do everything in his/her power to bring about the end of these cruel systems, and to ensure that every farm animal has the freedom to be able without difficulty, to turn round, groom itself, get up, lie down and stretch its limbs.

5) Support our campaign against cruelty to farm animals by becoming a member and sending for more information today.

Questions

1. What is the difference between a pressure group and a political party (3.1)?

2. Using data 3.2 to 3.4, list ways in which pressure groups try to influence those in power.

3. Pressure groups are essential to democracy. Briefly discuss this statement.

Coursework idea

Study a pressure group in your local area.
Investigate:
a) its aims,
b) the way it is organised,
c) how it attracts members,
d) the ways in which it trys to influence those in power.

Section 9
WORK

1 The meaning of work

Introduction

In modern industrial society a person's occupation is one of the most important factors in his or her life. It directly affects their status in society and therefore their self respect, their income and therefore their standard of living.

At one end of the scale people see their work as worthwhile, exciting and interesting, at the other end as worthless, dull and boring. This unit examines views about the meaning of work.

'Blessed is he'   1.1

Blessed is he who has found his work: let him ask no other blessedness.

Source: Thomas Carlyle 1795-1881

Why work?   1.2

The Bushmen live in the Kalahari Desert in Africa. Their traditional way of life was based on hunting and gathering wild fruit, nuts and vegetables. Work in terms of working fixed hours for a wage was unknown in their society. As one Bushman told a Western observer, 'Why should we work when we have mondogo nuts'.

Source: quote from T. Bilton et al *Introductory Sociology*

1.3

Fifty weeks here and two weeks at work would suit me better.

1.4

Off to work 1.5

Maureen and James Absalom live with their two young children and Maureen's mother in a four-bedroom house in Liverpool, which they rent for £17 a week. James, who had been unemployed for several years, accepted eventually that he could expect to find work only in the south. So he went to stay with Maureen's sister at Winchester, and took a job as a hospital porter on £87 a week (rising to £100 with overtime).

For the last five months he has seen his children only once every six to eight weeks, and has been searching hopelessly for affordable accommodation in one of the most expensive cities in the whole of southern England (a week's bed and breakfast in Winchester costs £70).

'If we don't do this, then we can never give our children anything better,' says Maureen Absalom. 'We are determined to make it work.'

Source: *Sunday Times Magazine*

Source: *Daily Mirror*

Questions

1. Briefly explain data 1.1 in your own words.
2. How does the Bushman (2.2) see the Western way of work?
3. a) Briefly explain the attitudes to work shown in data 1.3 and 1.4.

   b) Cartoons usually show the problems rather than the benefits of work. Why is this?
4. Judging from data 1.5, what does a job mean to James and Maureen Absalom?
5. Do you think there is any truth in the Andy Capp cartoon (1.6)? Explain your answer.

Coursework idea

Interview people in a variety of occupations (eg teacher, cleaner, electrician, accountant) about what work means to them and their reasons for working. Is there a connection between their occupation and their attitudes to work?

2 Job satisfaction

Introduction

Jobs can offer a number of rewards. A high status job can bring self respect. A well paid job brings many of the things that money can buy. A job seen as worthwhile can bring a sense of fulfilment. A job which allows a person to develop his or her talents can provide considerable satisfaction.

This unit looks at people's experience of work and asks what is it about the work itself which leads to more or less job satisfaction.

A furniture restorer 2.1

I won't say I exactly enjoy it. No, not enjoyment exactly but the time passes really quickly . . . what with so much to do, I just have to concentrate on the work. And it is satisfying - I have to say that . . . just to see, say, a chair, looking lovely, and knowing what it came in like. Yes, the money is important, stands to reason but I wouldn't change to some factory job to just earn more. No.

Source: S. Moore, *Sociology Alive*

Working for Ford 2.2

They decide on their measured day how fast we will work. They seem to forget that we're not machines. The standards they work to are excessive anyway. They expect you to work the 480 minutes of the eight hours you're on the clock. They've agreed to have a built-in allowance of six minutes for going to the toilet, blowing your nose and that. It takes you six minutes to get your trousers down.

Source H. Beynon, *Working for Ford*

2.3

'I find it stops them getting too bored.'

Working for Littlewoods 2.4

Although I could be called a clerical worker, it's just like being in a factory really. There are hundreds in my room and that's only one of many. The work is boring, repetitive and routine.

Source: pools clerk, Liverpool

Working for Big Mac   2.5

McDonald's secret recipe for success comes not from the Big Mac sauce but from a new production process, using a combination of the Fordist conveyor belt with a Japanese emphasis on flexibility. Each store is a factory where workers' skills have been eliminated and labour costs kept to a bare minimum. No chefs, no apprentices wanted on this burgerline: everyone has been levelled down to the uniform 'crew member' rushing between stations to perform tasks learnt in a day. Computerised machines do the cooking for you and regulate your movements to the second; the stated aim is to 'take the guesswork out of cooking.' From Oxford Street to Manila, McDonald's workers follow identical steps to produce identical burgers.

Source: *New Society, 9.10.87*

Cadbury's eggs   2.6

Automation has meant promotion for Paula Eadon. She used to work on the old production line wrapping hundreds of cream eggs a day. Now she's in charge of a computer that controls the flow of chocolate and cream.
'The wrapping machine was dead boring. Just sitting on that same old machine feeding the eggs in all the time. Now it's brilliant . . . you have to use your initiative and use your brains.'

Source: BBC TV *Nine till Five, February 1989*

Money isn't everything   2.7

There is job rotation. But to rotate is to temporarily change one kind of detailed labour for another; one hour of weighing; another hour of weighing on the opposite side of the machine (and the scales are all slightly different, in sensitivity or in speed of response); an hour of labelling and boxing. It's this last hour that brings a tea break, for the ninth girl is 'spare' (and the three take it in turn). She snatched maybe 15 minutes in the tea bay for a drink, a chat and a fag. Then an hour of weighing. Then 11.57 till 12.57, the dinner break. Maybe the daily shopping. Then the afternoon of weighing, labelling, weighing, weighing.
But week in week out, month in month out, it all comes down to basically the same thing: 'The worst thing about being here is it's so boring. Money isn't everything, is it?'

Source: J. West, *The Factory Slaves*

𝒬uestions

1. Why wouldn't the furniture restorer (2.1) change to a factory job to earn more?
2. The workers at Ford (2.2) had little control over the way their work was organised. Why might lack of control reduce job satisfaction?
3. What point is the cartoon (2.3) making about assembly line work?
4. How much job satisfaction do you think the workers at McDonald's get? Give reasons for your answer.
5. Explain why Paula Eadon's new job (2.6) is 'brilliant' compared to her old one.
6. Why is the work described in data 2.7 'so boring'?

Coursework idea

Interview a small sample of people with different jobs (eg unskilled manual workers through to professionals). Ask them to give a detailed description of their work. Find out what they like and dislike about their jobs and assess their level of job satisfaction. Try to explain any connections you find between the type of work and the level of job satisfaction.

Introduction

Trade unions were formed to represent employees - to protect their jobs and to improve their working conditions, wages and benefits (eg holidays and sick pay).

In the UK between 1976 and 1986, the number of people belonging to a trade union fell by 15%. The biggest membership falls were in the traditional industrial unions such as the Transport and General Workers Union and the Iron and Steel Trades Confederation. By comparison, 'white collar unions' have shown only a small decline and, in some cases, an increase in membership.

This unit looks at some of the possible reasons for the decline in trade union membership.

Union members (UK) 3.1

	thousands
1978	13112
1979	13289
1980	12947
1981	12106
1982	11593
1983	11236
1984	10994
1985	10716
1986	10333
1987	10200

Source: *Social Studies Review* March 1989

Unemployment rate: annual averages 3.2

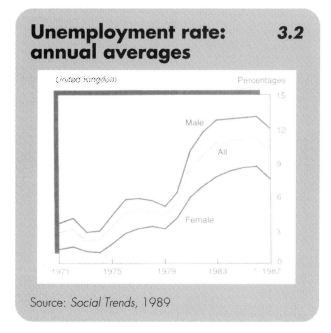

Source: *Social Trends*, 1989

Manufacturing and non-manufacturing employees in employment 3.3

Source: *Social Trends*, 1989

3.4

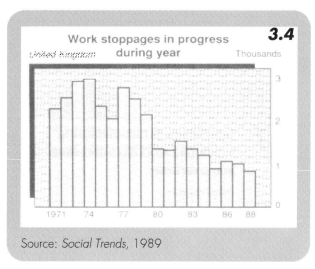

Work stoppages in progress during year

Source: *Social Trends*, 1989

Austin Rover assembly line

Questions

1. Compare the trend in trade union membership (3.1) with the unemployment rate (3.2).

   a) There appears to be a connection. Briefly describe it.

   b) Suggest a possible reason for the connection.

2. Traditionally most trade union members were manual workers. Bearing this in mind, can data 3.3 help to explain the decline in union membership? Give reasons for your answer.

3. Data 3.4 shows the number of strikes from 1971 to 1988.

   a) Describe the trend.

   b) Can you suggest a reason for this trend in view of data 3.2?

4. Use data 3.5 to provide one reason for the trend shown in data 3.3.

5. According to data 3.6, why will the decline in union membership continue?

The future?   3.6

In 10 years there will be more than 700,000 electronics engineers in Britain. More than half will be women. They will have an annual salary 30% bigger than now, even after allowing for inflation; on average, they will take home, after tax, the equivalent of what £16,000 would buy today, for working a maximum of 35 hours a week.

They will have the money to enjoy seven weeks' holidays a year, at least one of which will be spent abroad. When they are at home, each family will have the use of two cars and live in a house worth at least £130,000.

Unemployment will not be much of a worry and they are unlikely to want to become members of a traditional trade union. They will be attracted not by ideas of solidarity and collective action but pensions, investment advice and fitness clubs. This is the picture of the next decade painted by the Henley Centre for Forecasting. It is very different from what used to be considered the normal view of Britain's workforce. But since the height of union power during the winter of discontent in 1978/79, the profile of Britain's workforce has changed, with the gulf between skilled and unskilled widening dramatically.

'Skilled workers will enjoy a quite substantial increase in purchasing power,' says Professor Paul Ormerod of the Henley Centre. 'Their perception of class will be much weaker. Class solidarity for them will be non-existent.'

Source: *The Times*, 4.9.89

Coursework idea

Choose a sample of men and women in a variety of jobs. Ask whether or not they are members of a trade union. Find out their reasons for joining or not joining and their attitudes to trade unions in general. Is there a link between these factors and the type of job they hold? If so try to discover reasons for the link.

Introduction

A housewife is a strange occupational role - the employee is married to the employer. Housework is a peculiar type of work - it is not paid for. However there is little doubt that housework is seen as work by those who perform it.

This unit looks at the occupational role of the housewife and the nature of housework.

4.1

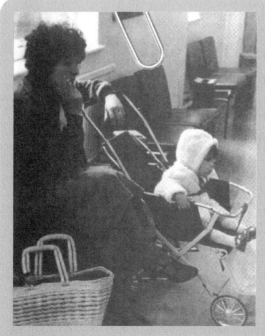

OCCUPATION: HOUSEWIFE

JOB DESCRIPTION: You will be expected to 'live in' at place of work and provide cleaning, cooking, shopping, laundry, nursing, teaching, entertainment and secretarial services for other inmates.

HOURS: You will be 'on call' 24 hours a day, 365 days a year. But your regular work will take between 50 and 100 hours per week.

PAYMENT: An allowance is available, known as 'house-keeping money' when provided by employer and 'family allowance' or 'child benefit' when provided by the State. This money is intended to cover essential expenses such as cleaning utensils and food. There is no payment for your labour as housewife.

HOLIDAYS: Your duties will be eased if your holiday is taken in a hotel, but you will often be expected simply to do your normal work in strange surroundings while other household members enjoy their leisure.

SATISFACTION: You may find your duties even more monotonous and under continuous time pressure than assembly-line workers. Seventy per cent of housewives in one study said they were 'very' or 'severely' dissatisfied with the nature of their work.

WORK HAZARDS: Insomnia, palpitations, headaches, dizziness, nightmares and anxiety ('housewives' syndrome') are much more common among housewives than women in paid employment.

JOB SECURITY: Your job will be continuously and increasingly threatened by divorce. If present trends continue, one in three marriages in Britain will end in divorce.

FRINGE BENEFITS: Your board and lodgings will usually be provided, but you will normally be expected to share a bedroom (and bed) with your employer.

Source: adapted from *New Internationalist*, March 1988

4.2

Price of a wife — £370 a week

Wives no longer feel insecure if you are at home, dependent on husband's earnings: you are probably worth £10,366 a year more than he is. So says Legal and General, the life assurance company, which has calculated your commercial worth.

The life assurers sent a team of pinstriped husbands out into the world to discover what it is you do. They reported back with a shock: wives work 92 hours a week, and labour to the value of £19,253 a year, rather more than the average male wage of £8,887.

Legal and General used employment agencies' fees to find out what it would cost to get a housewife's work (shopper, waitress, window cleaner, nurse, driver, cleaner, cook, child-minder, etc) done by someone else. The answer, according to a survey published today to coincide with mothering Sunday, is £370 a week.

That, by the way, is more than the salary of a bishop, a divisional fire chief, an army major or a Royal Marine captain with six years' service; a primary school head teacher or a second division footballer.

A typical week's work looked like this:	
28 hours childminding	£133
18 hours kitchen work (cooking etc)	£99.75
11 hours cleaning	£33
10 hours driving	£36
7 hours shopping	£16.80
Miscellaneous household tasks	£51.70
Total:	**£370.25**

Questions

1. a) No paid worker would accept the terms and conditions outlined in data 4.1. Do you agree? Give reasons for your answer.

    b) Briefly suggest why most housewives accept these terms and conditions.

2. a) Why is this picture (4.2) unusual?

    b) Do you think the scene it portrays should be repeated across the country? Give reasons for your answer.

3. a) Do you think the calculation of a housewife's worth (4.3) is reasonable? (These are 1987 figures so they need to rise with inflation).

    b) Should housewives be given a wage for housework? Explain your answer.

Coursework idea

Interview a number of housewives about whether or not they should be paid for housework.
Include in your sample:
a) those with full time paid employment
b) those with part time paid employment
c) those who are full time housewives
Do their responses differ?

5 Unemployment

Introduction

This unit looks at the experience of unemployment - what it feels like to be out of work. The first extract (5.1) was written in the 1930s by George Orwell, a middle class Englishman. Data 5.4 is an extract from the script of the BBC TV series *Boys from the Blackstuff* which was set in Liverpool.

The shame   5.1

When I first saw unemployed men at close quarters, the thing that horrified me was to find that many of them were *ashamed* of being unemployed . . . I remember the shock of astonishment it gave me . . . to find that a fair proportion of these beings whom I had been taught to regard as cynical parasites were decent young miners and cotton workers . . . They had been brought up to work, and it seemed as if they were never going to have the chance of working again. In their circumstances it was inevitable, at first, that they should be haunted by a feeling of personal degradation. That was the attitude towards unemployment in those days: it was a disaster which happened to you as an individual and for which *you* were to blame.

Source: G. Orwell, *Road to Wigan Pier*

Once Ye Have Seen My Face, Ye Dare Not Mock

I do 'nothing'   5.2

People ask what you do and you say nothing and they say never mind and that's the end of the subject - nothing more to talk about. You might lie because you're embarrassed about it to try to cover up, and make excuses if they ask more. They look down on you as if you're a layabout, especially if they're working. You feel you're the only one because all your friends seem to have jobs. You get very lonely, and you have no topic of conversation. My boyfriend says, 'Why don't you get a job, at least you'd have something to talk about.'

At home it's really depressing. You tend to get moody and unsociable. You lose confidence in yourself so that when you do get an interview you don't expect to get the job. At first you feel angry but after a while you lose interest. People keep telling me to get married and have children but there's no point in that. You're really tied down then and you still have to go out to work.

Often your parents thinks it's easy to get a job, but it's not. You can go out virtually all day, tramping around, killing yourself, going for interviews and getting turned down. And all your parents say is, 'Oh, never mind, at least you've had an interview.' They're pushing you out all the time. My brother says to me, 'Why haven't you got a job? I've got one .' But there's many more jobs open to boys than to girls. Your mother says, 'Never mind, there'll be another,' but you feel like giving up because you're so rejected.

Source: 'Girls Are Powerful' from *Young Women's Writings From 'Spare Rib'* edited by S. Hemmings

'Boys from the Blackstuff'

14. Interior. The boys' bedroom. Day.

Kevin is fast asleep in his single bed. We hear Dixie bouncing up the stairs. The door opens. Dixie goes to the side of the bed.

DIXIE: Kevin. Come on, get up.

   Kevin mumbles as he is wakened.

DIXIE: D'you know what time it is?

KEVIN: Er . . . No. (*He yawns*).

DIXIE: It's quarter past twelve.

KEVIN: Is that all?

DIXIE: I want you to get up.

KEVIN: It's too early, Dad. Anyway, what is there to get up for?

   Dixie grabs the duvet and hurls it away from the bed.

DIXIE: Get up!

KEVIN: What d'you do that for?

DIXIE: Because y' a bloody disgrace, Kevin. You're not even tryin' any more.

KEVIN: Leave off, will y', just leave off.

DIXIE: Get y' clothes on an' get out an' look f' work.

KEVIN: There is none.

   They are both shouting.

DIXIE: There is none when y' lyin' in bed.

KEVIN: An' there's none when I'm walkin' up an' down the industrial estate neither! You know that - you've been there with me as well. I've been left school two-and-a-half years. I've been out of work for two of them, and I've never so much as had a bastard interview. (*Kevin punches his bed*). So don't give me no crap about lyin' in bed.

   Kevin gets off the bed, grabs the duvet, lies down and covers himself. Dixie seems set to explode further, but he can't find the words.

Source: Alan Bleasdale, *Boys from the Blackstuff*

Questions

1. Why was George Orwell shocked (5.1)?

2. What point is the cartoonist making in data 5.3 (from the 1930s)?

3. Why is the girl in data 5.2 embarrassed about being unemployed?

4. a) Why does Kevin (5.4) sleep in?

   b) Why does unemployment often lead to friction in families? Refer to data 5.2 and 5.4 in your answer.

Coursework idea

Interview a sample of young people and adults about their views on:
1) what it's like to be unemployed,
2) who's to blame for unemployment,
3) what can and should be done about unemployment.

Note, and try to explain, any patterns in your interview data, eg differences in views of those who have been unemployed and those who have not.

CRIME AND DEVIANCE

1 Crime, deviance and death

Introduction

Death is normal in the sense it happens to everybody. However, there are many different ways of dying. Some are seen as normal, others as abnormal, some as legal, others as illegal.

Definitions of death vary from time to time and place to place. This unit examines ways of dying in order to show that whether or not an act is considered deviant or criminal depends on the situation, the time and the society.

Ancient Greece   *1.1*

Whoever no longer wishes to live shall state his reasons to the Senate, and after having received permission shall abandon life. If your existence is hateful to you, die; if you are overwhelmed by fate, drink the hemlock. If you are bowed with grief, abandon life. Let the unhappy man recount his misfortune, let the magistrate supply him with the remedy, and his wretchedness will come to an end.

Source: Montaigne, *Ancient Greece*

Justice?   *1.2*

A man was hanged who had cut his throat, but who had been brought back to life. They hanged him for suicide. The doctor had warned them that it was impossible to hang him as the throat would burst open and he would breathe through the aperture. They did not listen to his advice and hanged their man. The wound in the neck immediately opened and the man came back to life again although he was hanged. It took time to convoke the aldermen to decide the question of what was to be done. At length aldermen assembled and bound up the neck below the wound until he died.

Source: A. Alvarez, The Savage God

1.3

"I thought Norman had been looking a bit depressed lately."

Aztec society

Human sacrifice was common in Aztec society in Mexico. Those who died in this way included both Aztecs and their enemies captured in battle. For a warrior it was the most noble form of death. It is claimed that in 1486, 20,000 people were sacrificed in four days at the dedication of the great temple to the war god at Tenochtitlan.

The sacrifices were sometimes followed by ceremonial cannibalism. Parts of the dead person were eaten by members of the supreme council and the nobles. They believed that by eating human flesh the life force of the dead person would enter their bodies and give them strength to carry out the wishes of the gods.

Source: adapted from P. Tannahill, *Flesh and Blood*

Aztec sacrifice

Cannibalism   1.5

A plane carrying a group of Argentinian rugby players crashed in the Andes mountains in South America. They had run out of food.

★ ★ ★ ★ ★

'It's not going to be easy getting out of here,' said Canessa.

'But if we aren't rescued, we'll have to walk out,' said Fito.

'We'd never make it,' said Canessa. 'Look how weak we've become without food.'

'Do you know what Nando said to me?' Carlitos said to Fito. 'He said that if we weren't rescued, he'd eat one of the pilots to get out of here.' There was a pause; then Carlitos added, 'That hit on the head must have made him slightly mad.'

'I don't know,' said Fito, his honest, serious features quite composed. 'It might be the only way to survive.'

Inside there was silence. The boys cowered in the plane. Canessa told them that the meat was there on the roof, drying in the sun, and that those who wished to do so should come out and eat it. No one came, and again Canessa took it upon himself to prove his resolution. He prayed to God to help him do what he knew to be right and then took a piece of meat in his hand. He hesitated. Even with his mind so firmly made up, the horror of the act paralysed him. His hand would neither rise to his mouth nor fall to his side while the revulsion which possessed him struggled with his stubborn will. The will prevailed. The hand rose and pushed the meat into his mouth. He swallowed it.

He felt triumphant. His conscience had overcome a primitive, irrational taboo. He was going to survive.

Source: P. Reid, *Alive*

"What's your name? I need it for the menu."

Euthanasia 1.7

Frank Hanhart is an outdoor man. He lives for the pleasures of a small shoot he manages in his native Holland, and for his fly-fishing expeditions to England and Germany. The love of his life is his gun dog Bonnie, a seven-year-old springer spaniel. He bought her in Suffolk and refers to her as 'my English bitch'.

A year ago, Frank, aged 68, visited his doctor to discuss a routine prostate operation. Tests showed that he had extensive cancer. A nine-inch tumour under his left kidney was removed straight away, but a second tumour over the adrenal gland on his right side was inoperable. Frank is not prepared to endure a humiliating and painful death. He plans to end his life by swallowing a lethal dose of barbiturates made available to him by his GP. In Holland, euthanasia is permitted provided doctors follow state-approved guidelines.

'I'm not afraid of death. What worries me is the dying process. Being in a coma, you are not human any more. Then there's all the suffering and being in hospital, maybe for six months, and dying in a strange place. I've seen terminal patients in hospital and said that I would never, ever go that way. I've talked these things through with my doctor, my wife and my children. I had to make the point several times to my doctor that there was a standard of life below which I would not go. I know that when the time comes, he will give me the pills. My wife and children support me in this. We've had many talks about it. The important thing is that if they really love you, they won't want to see you suffer, they won't hold you here against your will.

'I don't look forward to dying, but I don't dread it. My main hope is to die in my house and say goodbye to my wife, my children and all the people I love. I want to swallow the pills myself. I want to take full responsibility for my death. And I want to do it knowing I am ready to leave, and in a way that shows respect for my body. I could take one of my guns right now and make a mess of it - but that's not the way.'

Source: *Observer Magazine*

Salvation Army, December 1914 1.8

[*A dreadful aircraft hangar of a place with bunks at either side of the large room, and bench after bench filling the rest of the space.*

We see TOPLIS *and the remnants of society.*

Many old tramps with unkempt beards, but a lot of younger people. A vacancy of expression.

They are lectured to by a Salvation Army captain]

CAPTAIN: . . . And so, as this, the first Christmas of the war against Germany approaches, as we meet here today in prayer, as I look around me at those of us who are in difficult circumstances, and as our brave boys fight on foreign fields, I want you to know one thing, gentlemen. There is no Christian sin in volunteering! The blame for this war does not rest with us! Germany forced this war and will undoubtedly be punished by God. The Lord is with our armies. Our cause is right. And right must triumph over might. Yes, do not forget what the Hun had already achieved in the cause of the Devil - the shameless murder of women and children! And so I ask you, those of you who are able-bodied men, who think that perhaps life has no purpose left, who have fallen on hard times, I ask you to consider that this is the time to do your duty! Now is the time for Christians to take up the sword! [*a short benign pause*] It is but a short walk with our sergeant here, a march even, to the recruiting office in Mosspits Lane.

[*And nothing happens*]

Meanwhile, if we would all join together, before soup is served, in the singing of that most beautiful of all hymns, 'Abide with Me'.

[*We see* TOPLIS *stand up. The* CAPTAIN *smiles at him, whispers loud enough for the whole room to hear*]

CAPTAIN: Brave man!

TOPLIS: I'm going to the lavatory, what's brave about that?

[*Laughter from the others.* TOPLIS *grins at them as he walks away from them. The audience rises*]

Source: A. Bleasdale, *The Monocled Mutineer*

THE SENTRY CAME UP INTO THE AIM BUT DAN BEAT HIM TO THE TRIGGER BY A SPLIT SECOND. **1.9**

Source: *Commando* (war comic)

An INLA funeral 1.10

Members of the Irish National Liberation Army

A Nazi concentration camp 1.11

Questions

1. Suicide is no longer illegal in the UK. However, helping a person commit suicide is illegal. Would the magistrate in ancient Greece (1.1) be acting illegally in terms of the law in Britain today? Give reasons for your answer.

2. In terms of today's standards in the UK who would you see as the wrongdoer - the man who attempted suicide or the alderman (1.2)? Explain your answer.

3. The cartoon (1.3) shows two kinds of suicide. What makes one kind deviant and the other normal in lemming society?

4. Explain why the Aztecs (1.4) and the Argentinian rugby players (1.5) reacted differently to cannibalism.

5. Why do we joke about things we consider deviant and morally offensive? Refer to cartoon 1.6 in your answer.

6. Killing or helping to kill a person may be seen as lawful or unlawful, good or bad, depending on the situation and the society. Discuss this statement using data 1.7 to 1.9.

7. Organisations such as the IRA and INLA (1.10) may be defined as 'terrorists' or 'freedom fighters'. One definition justifies the deaths they cause, the other does not. Briefly explain how the deaths they cause can be seen in two different ways.

8. Those in charge of Nazi concentration camps (1.11) said they were not criminals because they were 'only following orders'. After the war Allies prosecuted them as 'war criminals'. Which view do you support? Give reasons for your answer.

Coursework idea

The law reflects public opinion. Does it? Try to answer this question by interviewing people about their views on a) suicide; b) euthanasia; c) capital punishment.

Introduction

How accurate are official statistics on crime? Are certain types of offences unlikely to appear in official statistics? Do newspapers accurately reflect the extent and pattern of crime in society? These are the questions examined in this unit.

Notifiable offences recorded by the police 2.1

England and Wales

1971	1,665,700
1977	2,636,500
1978	2,561,500
1979	2,536,700
1980	2,688,200
1981	2,963,800
1982	3,262,400
1983	3,247,000
1984	3,499,100
1985	3,611,900
1986	3,847,400
1987	3,892,200

Notifiable offences cover more serious offences for which a suspect would have to be tried either at magistrates' courts or the Crown Court.

Source: adapted from *Social Trends*, 1989

Type of offence 2.2

England and Wales

Notifiable offences recorded	
Violence against the person	141,000
Sexual offences	25,200
of which, rape and attempted rape	2,500
Burglary	900,100
Robbery	32,600
Drugs offences	7,100
Theft and handling stolen goods	2,052,000
of which, theft of vehicles	389,600
Fraud and forgery	133,000
Criminal damage	589,000
Other notifiable offences	12,200
Total notifiable offences	3,892,200

Source: adapted from *Social Trends*, 1989

Newspaper headlines 2.3

A day in the life of brutal Britain

Knife gang robs train passengers

Teenager raped girl of 8 after watching sex video

EVERY DAY

7 women are raped

39 sexually assaulted

99 violently assaulted

Middle class crime 2.4

When it comes to crime, middle class people tend to have certain protections; they're able to operate within the orbit of their occupations. They don't have to go out at night with their galoshes on and scale up a wall. They do it while they're working - undercover, as it were - whether it's stealing a few pens, which is almost acceptable to society, or by engaging in fraud. When I read these sorts of things, I become annoyed that people should suggest they be let off lightly. A fella who screws a car may be misguided, may be foolish, but they have betrayed a trust through sheer greed, y'know. If they get caught, I treat them exactly the same as anybody else. I think some policemen don't - 'Gosh, this fella's quite well-to-do!' 'Apply the Act to them,' I say, 'that's all you've got to do. We aren't here to moralise.'

Source: J. McClure, *Spike Island*

Sex offences 2.6

Most sex offences are never revealed; when revealed, most are either ignored or not reported; if reported, a large percentage are dismissed for lack of proof, and when proof is established many are dropped because of the pressure and humiliation forced on the victim and family by the authorities.

Source: S. Nelson, *Incest*

2.5

'As this aerial picture shows quite clearly - a kidney-shaped pool, a large block of garages, extensive stables and paddocks, far-reaching acreage . . .'

Source: *Daily Express*, 24.5.88

Questions

1. a) Briefly describe the trend shown in table 2.1.
   b) Can these statistics be accepted as valid (true) measurement of crime? Explain your answer.
2. According to data 2.2, which type of offence is most common and which is least common?
3. a) Judging from the headlines (2.3), do newspaper reports reflect the overall picture of crime (given in table 2.2)?
   b) Why do you think newspapers select certain crimes to report?
   c) Do you think newspapers are acting responsibly in their reporting of crime? Explain your answer.
4. There is evidence that considerable middle class or 'white collar' crime goes undetected. Why? Refer to data 2.4 in your answer.

5. Cartoon 2.5 refers to a 'crime without a victim'. Why do large numbers of such crimes *not* appear in official statistics?
6. The evidence suggests that only a small minority of sex offences (rape, incest, sexual assault) are reported to the police. Why are so few reported? Refer to data 2.6 in your answer.

Coursework idea

Interview a sample of adults asking them if they have been a victim of crime over the past 5 years. Ask whether or not they reported the crime/s to the police and their reasons for reporting and/or not reporting. Use your results to discuss the problems of the validity and reliability of statistics on crime.

3 Labelling

Introduction

We tend to see people in terms of stereotypes and apply labels to them. These labels, eg thief, define not only their status but also what kind of a person they are, eg a thief is dishonest and untrustworthy. When a person has been labelled, others tend to see and act towards him or her in terms of the label. This may encourage deviant or criminal behaviour, eg a person labelled as a thief might be refused employment and turn to crime.

This unit looks at labelling.

Labelled

I LIVE in a body labelled
'handicapped'
Stunted legs and arms askew
I live in a body I wouldn't have chosen
But then few of us do.

People say I'm brave
As though bravery were a choice
I learned early not to scream
For mine is an unheard voice.

The world is competitive
And I'm ill-equipped to compete
But I'm no less of a person
Because I'm not complete.

I live in a body labelled 'second-rate'
Though I feel second to none
When society knows the difference
Then my battle is won.
Roger McGough

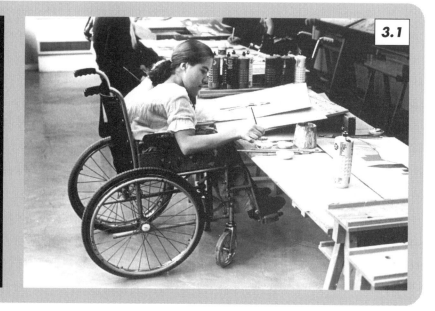

3.1

3.2

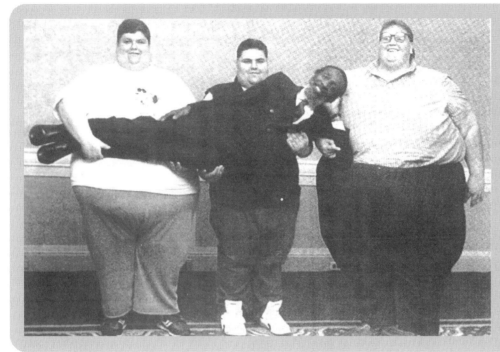

Ron Miller (37 stones), Lou Barone (26 stones) and Mike Parteleno (53 stones) with nutritionist Dick Gregory, who is helping them to diet

Football hooligans 3.4

The image of Britons overseas is now so bad that foreigners often fear our arrival, curse our presence and breathe a sigh of relief when we've gone.

This weekend as thousands of football fans streamed off cross-Channel ferries and converged on Stüttgart for England's opening match in the European Championships, they were greeted not with warm smiles and civic receptions but by squads of armed police and their fearsome dogs straining at the leash.

On Friday night in the Old Ascot Bar, the only English pub in Stüttgart, the vanguard of the English fans stood on tables chanting 'Zieg heil' and making Nazi salutes.

Sporting white T-shirts with 'Official English Hooligan' and 'English Invasion of Germany' emblazoned across their chests, many of them were clearly in the mood for trouble.

'It's going to be war,' said Michael, a scar-faced Chelsea fan.

Source: *Sunday Times*, 12.6.88

Questions

1. What point is the poet (3.1) making about labelling?
2. a) Why might the police be more likely to stop and search the youth in data 3.2 rather than a conventionally dressed youth?
   b) What effect might this have on the young man's future behaviour?
3. Look at photograph 3.3. To some extent it illustrates the stereotype of fat people. Describe this stereotype.
4. The media help to create labels which some people then try to live up to. Comment on this view using the newspaper report (3.4).

Coursework idea

Read a number of different newspapers over a period of three weeks. Collect examples of labels. Analyse the examples, compare the different newspapers and discuss how the papers might reinforce and/or create labels.

4 Causes of crime

Introduction

There is no single cause of crime. Explanations range from seeing the cause in individuals - their genetic makeup makes them more likely to commit crime; to the family - children have been inadequately socialised; to the peer group - a delinquent subculture which encourages crime; to society as a whole - the way society is organised puts pressure on certain members to turn to crime.

This unit looks at a number of explanations for criminal behaviour.

Dragonquest 4.1

Police in a small town north of Tokyo were called in last weekend to investigate a burglary in which a thief who entered a home through a lavatory window took neither money nor valuables. The only thing missing was a plastic case containing Dragonquest III, the latest version of an extremely difficult video game.

The burglary was one of seven crimes related to Dragonquest III in less than a week. There have been cases of extortion and theft as well, mostly involving high school students.

It is difficult to imagine any country other than Japan where children turn to crime to acquire a game which a person of average intelligence requires a week to decipher. Dragonquest is the most difficult of all video games marketed so far here.

Students in Japan's highly competitive schools vie to be the first to crack a particularly difficult new game. Being late in acquiring a Dragonquest III means being left behind in the race for popularity in school.

The crime wave - as well as the long queues of people wanting to buy the game - have been the result of a level of demand unforeseen by the manufacturer, a small Tokyo software company called Enix. Enix released one million Dragonquest sets on 10 February. All were sold before noon of that day.

At one Tokyo store some 10,000 people queued up for 3,000 tickets entitling them to buy one game each. Hundreds spent the night on the pavement in front of stores. As 10 February was a school day, parents took time off from work to queue up for school-age children. 'I cannot go home empty-handed,' said one father.

Just under 400 students were taken into custody throughout the country by truancy officers - and probably thousands of others got away. When television crews filmed the queues in front of electronics stores, most of those waiting hid their faces from cameras.

The crimes began almost immediately after 10 February when it became apparent that no more sets would be available for more than a week.

Source: *The Independent*

Professional criminals 4.2

'I suppose,' I said to John, as we made our way back from the Landsdowne one September evening, 'they're not *all* that different to accountants or stockbrokers. I can see what you mean about it being a job to them. They get up in the morning, or at least the afternoon, and go to work. Keep their eyes open. Look for openings. And just like other professional groups they pull together their own set of attitudes and ideas about what's right and wrong, about how to have a good time, how to treat their families and kids, how to look after other people who're in the same game.'

Source: L. Taylor, *Into the Underworld*

The delinquent subculture 4.3

Mike comes from the heart of white Cockney Hoxton, Britain's longest-standing traditional high-crime area with a reputation that dates back for centuries. An area where the Old Bill (the police) are regarded with respectful hostility, where fences tout from door to door offering anything from dresses to vacuum-cleaners or forged luncheon vouchers. And an area where many young white boys have their own distinctive subculture in which vandalism, petty crime, gang warfare and an often ugly racialism play a part.

Mike's career of lawless behaviour began when he was only nine, helping older friends to break into shops and lock-up garages. It was related, from the first, to educational failure. Failure on Mike's part to do well, failure on the school's part to hold his interest: 'I used to run out of primary school. The head of my house at secondary school said, "We can't do nothing with Michael," so they let me pick my own lessons. I only did four hours a week, cookery, motor engineering, and PE. The rest of the time I bunked off.'

Source: P. Harrison, *Inside the Inner City*

Drink and crime 4.4

Clear links between teenage drinking and crime are shown by an investigation in Mid-Glamorgan - the county with the worst crime rate in Britain.

The investigation was initiated by Mr. Nicholas Edwards, the Welsh Secretary, who is concerned about the county's crime figures. It discovered that one out of three teenagers currently on probation had been drinking before committing crimes - many of them heavily.

Based on interviews with 98 young offenders in the county aged between 14 and 20, the investigation shows seven out of ten of those who had been drinking had consumed more than four-and-a-half pints of beer. Some had drunk as many as 13 pints.

The investigation by the Mid-Glamorgan Crime Prevention Working Party - a joint local authority police body - found that seven out of ten youngsters interviewed said boredom was the main reason for breaking the law. Lack of money was also cited.

But the working party's biggest concern was the influence of alcohol, with many youngsters - often still at school - meeting in public houses before committing offences. 'Alcohol was the trigger in most of these cases,' said Mr. Alwyn Williams, working party chairman.

Source: *Times Educational Supplement*, 9.1.87

Questions

1. One of the most famous explanations for crime, put forward by Robert K. Merton, states that society defines people's 'wants' and 'desires'. If people cannot satisfy these wants by legal means, there will be pressure on them to turn to illegal means.

   a) How does this help to explain the Dragonquest crimes (4.1)?

   b) How can the example of Dragonquest be used to explain other types of crime?

2. Criminals are not very different from non-criminals. Discuss this statement with reference to data 4.2.

3. Mike was socialised into crime?

   a) Support this statement using data 4.3.

   b) Why might failure at school encourage Mike's delinquent behaviour?

4. 'Alcohol' was the trigger in most of these cases' (4.4). Explain this statement.

Coursework idea

Interview students in your school/college asking them:
a) to list the number of times they have broken the law,
b) their reasons for breaking the law.
Analyse their reasons and compare them with sociological explanations for crime.

5 Prisons

Introduction

Compared to the size of its population, Britain has the largest prison population in Europe. Prisons are supposed to deter people from committing crime, to punish and rehabilitate the inmates and to protect the public. In recent years, the steady rise in recorded crime, the growing prison population and the increasing costs of the prison service have led to calls for alternatives to prison.

This unit looks at some of the problems of prisons and some of the alternatives to prison.

Learning skills   5.1

Immature boys of 15 and 16 imprisoned in a youth custody centre alongside experienced criminals are being bullied and lured into corruption, according to a report yesterday by HM Chief Inspector of Prisons, Judge Stephen Tumim.

In a highly critical investigation into Werrington Youth Custody Centre, near Stoke-on-Trent, Judge Tumim describes a closed society where apathy and frustration are able to fester among inmates in depressing conditions.

It is a place where younger inmates 'learned the skills of house-breaking and other crimes from the older ones' and where 'tobacco barons' control the young and weak. The report says the inmates show a great deal of apathy and low expectation for the future.

'Many expected to return and to spend much of their future in prison and not to find employment outside.'

Mental illness   5.2

A leading psychiatrist said yesterday that the Government's policy of closing mental hospitals in favour of 'care in the community' simply means that growing numbers of mentally disturbed people are being sent to prison for offences such as stealing a pint of milk from a doorstep, riding on a train without paying, or stealing a pie because they are hungry.

Dr. Coid has studied all mentally abnormal men remanded by the courts to Winchester Prison for psychiatric reports in the five years between 1979 and 1983.

Of the 334 men studied, the overwhelming majority were schizophrenics. A total of 27 per cent had been arrested for offences 'carried out primarily to obtain food or shelter.

Many of these were pathetic minor incidents, involving hungry and destitute men, such as shoplifting food from supermarkets and pies and milk bottles from private houses.'

One schizophrenic 'burglar' was arrested for breaking into a village school where he was found by the children in the morning asleep under a desk.

5.3

TEHRAN
POLICE
DEPT.

CRIMINAL
RECORDS
OFFICE

"Yes, O High One, one previous conviction."

Alternatives

Persuading magistrates and the public that non-custodial schemes for young offenders are not a soft touch is a difficult task. But concern is growing over the re-offending rates of juveniles who are either taken into care or given a term in detention, and increasingly the courts are looking at alternatives to custody, such as the programmes run by social services and the probation service which provide strict supervision and attempts at rehabilitation.

The statistics are encouraging: the re-offending rate among those offered such programmes as the Bail Support Scheme, started by the Southwark Alternative to Custody Scheme two years ago, is 40 per cent while the rate for those sent to prison is between 70 and 80 per cent. Under the Southwark programme, of 48 children - three girls and 45 boys, aged between 13 and 17 facing charges ranging from attempted murder to an explosives charge, shoplifting and indecent assault - only four breached bail and one of them managed to stay out of trouble over a nine-month remand period. 'Eventually he got three years for "glassing" someone,' Steve James, leader of the scheme said.

'Although he had no previous convictions he is now in prison and what good is it doing him? Unfortunately he is learning the tricks of the trade. Under a supervision order with an intermediate treatment programme, we could have helped him. We could have prevented him from doing anything like that again.'

Source: *The Independent*, 17.2.89

Questions

1. Prison simply breeds apathy, frustration and more efficient criminals. What support does data 5.1 provide for this view?

2. The men in the study described in data 5.2 should not be in prison. Do you agree? Give reasons for your answer.

3. Consider the alternatives to prison in data 5.3 and 5.4. Do you think they would be a) effective; b) acceptable? Give reasons for your answer.

4. What support is provided for 'non-custodial schemes' (ie alternatives to custody) by data 5.5?

Coursework idea

Interview a number of experts - prison officers, probation officers, former prisoners - about prison and its success or lack of it.